BRITISH CAENOZOIC FOSSILS

(TERTIARY AND QUATERNARY)

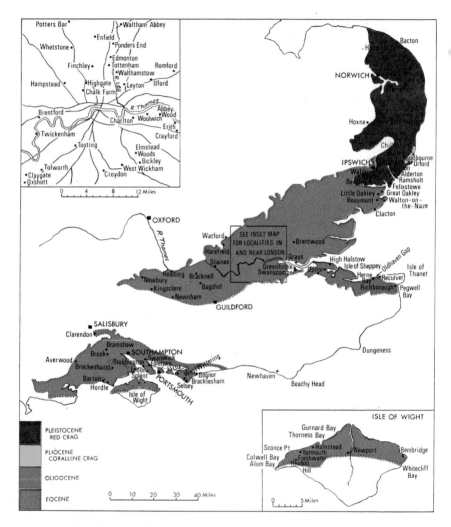

Distribution of Tertiary Strata and Quaternary Crag Deposits,
with the principal fossiliferous localities.
(Other Quaternary or Drift Deposits omitted.)

ρ

British Museum (Natural History)

BRITISH
CAENOZOIC FOSSILS

(TERTIARY AND QUATERNARY)

FOURTH EDITION

London

Trustees of the British Museum (Natural History)

1971

First Edition	.	.	.	1960
Second Edition	.	.	.	1963
Third Edition	.	.	.	1968
Fourth Edition	.	.	.	1971

Publication No. 540

S.B. No. 56500540 5

Printed in England by Staples Printers Limited at their Kettering, Northants, establishment

Contents

Preface to First Edition

This publication is the first of a series of handbooks illustrating British fossils which are being issued in response to repeated requests for a simple and inexpensive book to enable the young, or those without experience, to know what fossils they may expect to find, or, even more important from our point of view, to identify for themselves those they have collected.

The selection of species to be illustrated has presented considerable difficulty—whether a species is common or not is often a matter of opinion or of individual experience, depending very much on time and place. Clearly as many groups of animals and plants as practicable should be represented in our illustrations, in spite of the overwhelming preponderance (microscopic forms apart) of molluscs among British Caenozoic fossils; and naturally also there is in our choice considerable bias towards the kind of fossil most often brought into the Museum—and such fossils are by no means always those most commonly found. Three hundred and fifty-four Tertiary and Quaternary species, a very small proportion of the thousands recorded, are illustrated.

A selection of specimens illustrating this handbook is exhibited in the second bay of the Fossil Mammal Gallery. The specimens exhibited are indicated by an asterisk in the explanation of plates.

Fossils are not always so well preserved as many of the specimens selected for illustration, and the beginner is reminded that great care is always desirable in extracting fossils from the rock. Advice on collecting and preserving is given in the Museum's publication: *Instructions for Collectors, No. 11. Fossils, Minerals and Rocks.*

The first volume covers the fauna and flora of the Caenozoic era, that is, organisms that flourished during the last 60 million years or so,* from the beginning of the Eocene period up to the present day. The geography and general conditions of those times are not dealt with here, since they are discussed in some detail in the companion handbook *The Succession of Life through Geological Time.* This new volume is essentially a book for identifying fossils. By the start of the Caenozoic era most archaic animals and plants had been replaced by those of more modern aspect, and an increasing number of forms still living appear in the later Caenozoic periods. But for the mammals, the warm-blooded animals that

---

* The latest estimate of the duration of the Caenozoic era is 70 million years.

culminated in man, this was the great period of development and expansion. However, mammal remains, except for the almost modern types of the Pleistocene period, are, unfortunately, all too rare in this country.

Scientific nomenclature presents a most vexatious problem. Many names long familiar in text-books and the older scientific treatises have had to be altered as a result of re-assessment of the affinities of individual species or owing to the necessity, under international rules, of using the first names published. Those wishing to pursue this subject further are referred to p. 27.

The preparation of this series was initiated several years ago by my predecessor, the late W. N. Edwards, and was put into the capable hands of a distinguished amateur geologist and artist, Mr. A. G. Wrigley, whose untimely death, when some 60 drawings for this volume had been completed, stopped the project for a considerable time. When opportunity allowed, the work was handed over to Mr. C. P. Castell under the general supervision of Dr. L. R. Cox, F.R.S. Most of the figures not by Mr. Wrigley are the work of two other artists, Miss L. D. Buswell and Miss L. Ripley, but his style has been retained as far as possible. Some of Mr. Wrigley's illustrations, already published in the *Proceedings of the Malacological Society* and in the *Proceedings of the Geologists' Association*, have been utilized and thanks are due to the Councils of the two Societies for permission to reproduce the original drawings. Many of the scientific and experimental staff of the Department have helped in this compilation, but the bulk of the work has been carried out by Mr. Castell, and edited by the Deputy Keeper, Dr. H. M. Muir-Wood; the late Mr. A. G. Davis and Messrs. P. Cambridge, Dennis Curry and M. P. Kerney have given us valuable assistance.

Errol White,
5th December, 1958   *Keeper of Palaeontology*

Preface to Second Edition

This handbook has had the success that its authors expected, for with its companion volumes on the Mesozoic (now published) and the Palaeozic fossils (to be published next year) it fills a very obvious gap in geological literature.

The plates are unaltered and the text remains substantially the same, apart from some nomenclatorial titivation (largely as the result of Miss M. E. J. Chandler's admirable palaeobotanical researches), the addition of a time-scale and of plate references to the distribution lists.

Very little criticism of the volume has been received, but the few suggestions that have been made, chiefly by Dr. F. W. Anderson of H.M. Geological Survey, are incorporated.

ERROL WHITE,
Keeper of Palaeontology

26th October, 1962

Preface to Fourth Edition

Palaeontology, though a study of the dead, is very much a living science, as is evidenced by the need for a further edition of this handbook. The fourth edition includes a number of nomenclature emendations throughout the text, some of which are corrections but others arise from the recently completed researches of palaeontologists.

Further recent refinements in our knowledge of the past are incorporated in the newly-revised time-scale.

April 1971

H. W. BALL
Keeper of Palaeontology

Introduction

Fossils are the remains or traces of animals and plants preserved in the rocks of the earth's crust. The vast length of time (estimated at about 600 million years) that has elapsed since the deposition of the oldest rocks containing unmistakable remains of organisms is subdivided into the Palaeozoic, Mesozoic and Caenozoic eras. The Caenozoic era, which began about 70 million years ago and still continues, is divided into the Eocene, Oligocene, Miocene, Pliocene, Pleistocene and Holocene periods, the first four of which are frequently grouped together as the Tertiary era, and the Pleistocene and Holocene as the Quaternary. Agreement has only recently been reached as to where the dividing line between Pliocene and Pleistocene, or the upper limit of the Tertiary, should be drawn. Tables showing the classification of British Caenozoic rocks are on pp. 3, 4.

The rocks of Eocene and Oligocene age are almost confined to south-eastern England (see map), their outcrops being situated mainly in two areas, the London and Hampshire Basins. There are now few places in London or its near vicinity where good collections of fossils can be obtained, although temporary exposures of underlying strata always deserve attention. Further afield in Kent, the cliffs and beach near Herne Bay still yield abundant specimens from the Thanet Sands, Woolwich Beds and Blackheath Beds, while London Clay fossils can be found at Sheppey. In the Hampshire Basin many fossils from the London Clay and Bracklesham Beds can be obtained from the foreshore at low tide at Bognor Regis and at Bracklesham respectively, when the rocks are not obscured by overlying sand, while well-preserved fossil shells abound in the Upper Eocene beds at Barton. In the north-west of the Isle of Wight the cliffs of Alum Bay, Headon Hill and Colwell Bay yield many fossils from formations ranging in age from Lower Eocene to Oligocene, while good collections from still higher beds of the Oligocene may be made east of Yarmouth. The cliffs at Whitecliff Bay, on the north-eastern side of the island, are also rich in Eocene and Oligocene fossils. At Bovey Tracey, Devon, is an isolated patch of Oligocene clays containing plant remains; while on the Island of Mull, off the west coast of Scotland, an important warm-temperate flora of Eocene age has been found, but of this no adequate description yet exists.

Rocks generally accepted as Miocene in age are absent in Great Britain. The 'Crag' of East Anglia consists of shelly sands ranging in age from

1

Pliocene to Lower Pleistocene, and contains many well-preserved fossils. It is no longer possible, however, to collect from the isolated exposure of Pliocene beds at St. Erth in Cornwall, from which many shells were once obtained. Fossiliferous Pleistocene deposits of younger age than the Crag of East Anglia and the still later Holocene deposits are partly of marine and partly of non-marine origin, and are so scattered that there is not always clear evidence of their relative ages. Moreover, many of these deposits have been exposed only in temporary sections. The marine deposits include raised beaches and various patches of shelly gravels, and their fossils belong largely, although not entirely, to living species. The fluviatile and other non-marine deposits are of interest as containing, among other fossils, remains of mammalia which lived in this country during the Ice Ages or during the intervening interglacial periods. Strictly speaking, human artefacts preserved in gravels and other deposits are to be regarded as fossils, but no illustrations of these are included in the present handbook, as such remains are dealt with in the Museum publication, *Man the Tool-maker*, by K. P. Oakley.

L.R.C.

Stratigraphical Tables
of
British Caenozoic Formations

Lower Caenozoic (Lower Tertiary)

OLIGOCENE

Stage	Formation	Important Localities for Fossils
Chattian	[Absent]	
Rupelian (=Stampian)	?Bovey Tracey Plant Beds	Bovey Tracey.
	Upper Hamstead Beds	Hamstead.
	Lower Hamstead Beds	Yarmouth, I. of Wight, to Hamstead
	Bembridge Marls	Yarmouth to Hamstead. Gurnard Bay; Whitecliff Bay.
Lattorfian (=Sannoisian)	Bembridge Limestone	Headon Hill; Sconce Point; Hamstead Ledge; quarries near Freshwater; White-cliff Bay.
	Osborne Beds	Headon Hill; Whitecliff Bay.
	Middle and Upper Headon Beds	Headon Hill to Colwell Bay; Whitecliff Bay; Hordle; Brockenhurst.

EOCENE

Stage			Formation	Important Localities for Fossils
UPPER EOCENE	Bartonian		Lower Headon Beds	Headon Hill to Colwell Bay; Whitecliff Bay; Hordle.
			Barton Beds and Hengistbury Beds	Barton; Alum Bay; White-cliff Bay.
MIDDLE EOCENE	Auversian		Upper Bracklesham Beds and ?Bourne-mouth Marine Beds and Boscombe Sands	Selsey; Whitecliff Bay; Brook; Bramshaw; Hill Head, Lee-on-Solent.
	Lutetian		Lower Bracklesham Beds (upper part) and ?Bournemouth Freshwater Beds	Whitecliff Bay; Brackle-sham; Selsey; Southampton.
LOWER EOCENE	Cuisian		Lower Bracklesham Beds (lower part)	Whitecliff Bay; East Wittering.
			Lower Bagshot Sands	Alum Bay.
			Pipe-clay Series	Poole Harbour.
	Ypresian		London Clay	London area generally; Oxshott; Sheppey; Bognor; Alum Bay; Whitecliff Bay.
			London Clay Basement Beds	Harefield.
	Sparnacian		Blackheath Beds (= Oldhaven Beds)	Abbey Wood; Bishopstone (near Herne Bay).
			Woolwich and Reading Beds	Charlton, Bishopstone.
	Thanetian		Thanet Sands	Reculver and Bishopstone; Pegwell Bay.
	Montian		[Absent]	

4

Upper Caenozoic (Upper Tertiary and Quaternary)

(The classification of some Pleistocene formations is still uncertain)

HOLOCENE

Terrestrial and marine deposits formed less than 10,000 years ago (i.e. from Mesolithic times onward). Examples: many deposits of gravel, alluvium and peat; submerged forests; tufas; blown sand; etc.

PLEISTOCENE

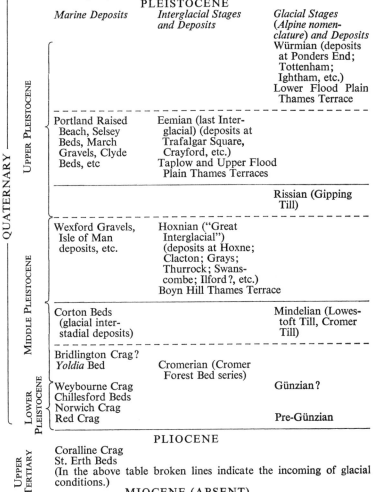

	Marine Deposits	*Interglacial Stages and Deposits*	*Glacial Stages (Alpine nomenclature) and Deposits*
			Würmian (deposits at Ponders End; Tottenham; Ightham, etc.) Lower Flood Plain Thames Terrace
UPPER PLEISTOCENE	Portland Raised Beach, Selsey Beds, March Gravels, Clyde Beds, etc	Eemian (last Interglacial) (deposits at Trafalgar Square, Crayford, etc.) Taplow and Upper Flood Plain Thames Terraces	
			Rissian (Gipping Till)
MIDDLE PLEISTOCENE	Wexford Gravels, Isle of Man deposits, etc.	Hoxnian ("Great Interglacial") (deposits at Hoxne; Clacton; Grays; Thurrock; Swanscombe; Ilford ?, etc.) Boyn Hill Thames Terrace	
	Corton Beds (glacial interstadial deposits)		Mindelian (Lowestoft Till, Cromer Till)
LOWER PLEISTOCENE	Bridlington Crag? *Yoldia* Bed	Cromerian (Cromer Forest Bed series)	
	Weybourne Crag Chillesford Beds Norwich Crag Red Crag		Günzian? Pre-Günzian

QUATERNARY

PLIOCENE

Coralline Crag
St. Erth Beds
(In the above table broken lines indicate the incoming of glacial conditions.)

MIOCENE (ABSENT)

5

Geological Distribution of the Species illustrated

The numbers appended to the name of each species refer to the plate and figure which illustrate it. If the specimen illustrated is from a different geological formation this reference is placed in square brackets.

EOCENE
THANET SANDS (INCLUDING CORBULA BED)

Bivalvia   *Arctica morrisi* (J. de C. Sowerby), [11, 4, 5]
Astarte tenera Morris, 9, 2, 3
Corbula regulbiensis Morris, 14, 11–13
Cucullaea decussata Parkinson, 7, 6, 7
Cyrtodaria rutupiensis (Morris), 15, 11, 12
Dosiniopsis bellovacina (Deshayes), 13, 9–11
Eutylus cuneatus (Morris), 16, 4
Garum edvardsi (Morris), 15, 5
Nemocardium plumstedianum (J. Sowerby), [12, 10, 11]
Ostrea bellovacina Lamarck, [8, 4, 5]
Panopea intermedia (J. Sowerby), [16, 5]
Thracia oblata (J. de C. Sowerby), 15, 1

Gastropoda   *Euspira bassae* Wrigley, 18, 5, 6
Sigatica abducta (Deshayes), [18, 1]
Siphonalia subnodosa (Morris), [22, 2, 3]

Pisces   *Striatolamia striata* (Winkler), [28, 3]
Lamna obliqua (Agassiz), [28, 1]

WOOLWICH AND READING BEDS

Brachiopoda   *Discinisca ferroviae* Muir-Wood, 3, 5

Bivalvia   *Arctica planata* (J. de C. Sowerby), [11, 7]
Corbicula cordata (Morris), 10, 11, 12
Corbicula cuneiformis (J. Sowerby), 10, 6–8
Corbicula (*Tellinocyclas*) *tellinoides* (Férussac), [10, 4, 5]
Cucullaea decussata Parkinson, [7, 6, 7]
Glycymeris plumstediensis (J. Sowerby), [5, 10]

7

8   *British Caenozoic Fossils*

Nemocardium plumstedianum (J. Sowerby), [**12**, 10, 11]
Ostrea bellovacina Lamarck, [**8**, 4, 5]
Ostrea tenera J. Sowerby, [**8**, 3]
Pitar (Calpitaria) obliquus (Deshayes), [**13**, 12, 13]
Teredina personata (Lamarck), [**16**, 1–3]

Gastropoda *Brotia melanioides* (J. Sowerby), **19**, 13, 14
Calyptraea aperta (Solander), [**17**, 10]
Melanopsis antidiluviana (Poiret), [**19**, 8]
Pseudoliva fissurata (Deshayes), [**22**, 1]
Siphonalia subnodosa (Morris), [**22**, 2, 3]
Tympanotonos funatus (J. Sowerby), **19**, 5

Pisces *Amia* sp., [**30**, 3]
Lamna obliqua (Agassiz), [**28**, 1]
Striatolamia striata (Winkler), [**28**, 3]
Squatina prima (Winkler), [**28**, 10]
Phyllodus toliapicus Agassiz, [**30**, 1]

BLACKHEATH BEDS (INCLUDING OLDHAVEN BEDS)

Brachiopoda *Discinisca ferroviae* Muir-Wood, [**3**, 5]

Bivalvia *Arctica morrisi* (J. de C. Sowerby), **11**, 4, 5
Corbicula cuneiformis (J. Sowerby), [**10**, 6–8]
Corbicula (Tellinocyclas) tellinoides (Férussac), **10**, 4, 5
Dosiniopsis bellovacina (Deshayes), [**13**, 9–11]
Glycymeris plumstediensis (J. Sowerby), **5**, 10
Nemocardium plumstedianum (J. Sowerby), **12**, 10, 11
Nucula fragilis Deshayes, **5**, 3, 4
Ostrea bellovacina Lamarck, **8**, 4, 5
Ostrea tenera J. Sowerby, **8**, 3
Pitar (Calpitaria) obliquus (Deshayes), **13**, 12, 13
Pteria media (J. Sowerby), [**6**, 7]

Gastropoda *Aporrhais triangulata* Gardner, **20**
Brotia melanioides (J. Sowerby), [**19**, 13, 14]
Euspira bassae Wrigley, **18**, 5, 6
Euspira glaucinoides (J. Sowerby), [**18**, 2]
Hastula plicatula (Lamarck), **26**, 14, 15

Melanopsis antidiluviana (Poiret), **19**, 8
Pseudoliva fissurata (Deshayes), **22**, 1
Sigatica abducta (Deshayes), **18**, 1
Siphonalia subnodosa (Morris), **22**, 2, 3
Tympanotonos funatus (J. Sowerby), [**19**, 5]

Pisces   *Acipenser* sp., [**29**, 4]
Albula eppsi White & Frost, [**30**, 4]
Amia sp., **30**, 3
Hypolophus sylvestris White, **29**, 3
Lamna obliqua (Agassiz), [**28**, 1]
Lepisosteus suessionensis Gervais, **30**, 5
Odontaspis (Synodontaspis) teretidens White, **28**, 2
Striatolamia striata (Winkler), **28**, 3
Phyllodus toliapicus Agassiz, **30**, 1
Squatina prima (Winkler), **28**, 10
Physodon secundus (Winkler), [**28**, 5]

LONDON CLAY

Plantae   *Anonaspermum rotundatum* Reid & Chandler, **1**, 1
Chara medicaginula (Lamarck), [**1**, 11]
Cinnamomum globulare Reid & Chandler, **1**, 10
Hightea elliptica Bowerbank, **1**, 13
Hightea turgida Bowerbank, **1**, 14, 15
Iodes corniculata Reid & Chandler, **1**, 2
Magnolia lobata (Bowerbank), **1**, 3
Nipa burtini (Brongniart), **1**, 18
Oncoba variabilis (Bowerbank), **1**, 4, 5
Petrophiloides richardsoni Bowerbank, **1**, 16
Wetherellia variabilis Bowerbank, **1**, 7, 8

Protozoa   *Marginulina wetherelli* Jones, **2**, 3

Coelenterata   *Paracyathus crassus* Edwards & Haime, **3**, 9

ECHINODERMA

Echinoderma   *Archastropecten crispatus* (Forbes), **4**, 5
Isselicrinus subbasaltiformis (Miller), **4**, 8, 9
Ophiura wetherelli Forbes, **4**, 7

Annelida   *Ditrupa plana* (J. Sowerby), **3**, 7
Rotularia bognoriensis (Mantell), **3**, 8

Brachiopoda   *Lingula tenuis* J. Sowerby, **3**, 4
Terebratula hantonensis Muir-Wood, **3**, 1, 2
Terebratulina wardenensis Elliott, **3**, 3

Bivalvia   *Abra splendens* (J. de C. Sowerby), **14**, 6
Amusium (*Lentipecten*) *corneum* (J. Sowerby), [**7**, 5]
Arctica morrisi (J. de C. Sowerby), [**11**, 4, 5]
Arctica planata (J. de C. Sowerby), **11**, 7
Astarte filigera S. V. Wood, **9**, 4
Callista (*Microcallista*) *proxima* (Deshayes), **13**, 4–6
Cucullaea decussata Parkinson, [**7**, 6, 7]
Cultellus affinis (J. Sowerby), **14**, 2
Dosiniopsis bellovacina (Deshayes) [Basement Bed],
[**13**, 9–11]
Glycymeris brevirostris (J. de C. Sowerby), **5**, 9
Glycymeris plumstediensis (J. Sowerby), [**5**, 10]
Glycymeris wrigleyi Curry, **6**, 1, 2
Musculus elegans (J. Sowerby), **6**, 3, 4
Nemocardium nitens (J. Sowerby), **11**, 6
Nemocardium plumstedianum (J. Sowerby) [Basement Bed]
[**12**, 10, 11]
Nuculana amygdaloides (J. de C. Sowerby), **5**, 5, 6
Panopea intermedia (J. Sowerby), **16**, 5
Pecten duplicatus J. de C. Sowerby, **7**, 3, 4
Pholadomya margaritacea (J. Sowerby), **16**, 6
Pinna affinis J. Sowerby, **7**, 1
Pitar (*Calpitaria*) *obliquus* (Deshayes) [Basement Bed],
[**13** 12, 13]
Pitar (*Calpitaria*) *sulcatarius* (Deshayes), **13**, 1–3
Pteria media (J. Sowerby), **6**, 7
Teredina personata (Lamarck), **16**, 1–3
Thracia oblata (J. de C. Sowerby), [**15**, 1]
Thyasira angulata (J. Sowerby), **12**, 9
Thyasira goodhalli (J. de C. Sowerby), **12**, 12

Gastropoda   *Aporrhais sowerbii* (Fleming), **20**, 5, 6
Aporrhais triangulata Gardner [Basement Bed], [**20**, 1]
Athleta (*Volutospina*) *denudatus* (J. de C. Sowerby), **25**, 5
Athleta (*Volutospina*) *nodosus* (J. de C. Sowerby), **25**, 7
Bonellitia laeviuscula (J. Sowerby), **26**, 4
Calyptraea aperta (Solander), [**17**, 10]
Eopleurotoma simillima (Edwards), **26**, 19

Euspira glaucinoides (J. Sowerby), **18**, 2
Euthriofusus complanatus (J. de C. Sowerby), **24**, 4
Euthriofusus transversarius Wrigley, **24**, 2
Ficus (Priscoficus) multiformis Wrigley, **21**, 2, 3
Ficus (Priscoficus) smithi (J. de C. Sowerby), **21**, 6
Fusinus wetherelli Wrigley, **23**, 12
Galeodea gallica Wrigley, **21**, 4
Hippochrenes amplus (Solander), [**20**, 10]
Orthochetus elongatus Wrigley, **19**, 1
Pollia londini (Wrigley), **23**, 1
Pseudoliva fissurata (Deshayes), [**22**, 1]
Pseudoneptunea curta (J. de C. Sowerby), **24**, 6
Sigatica abducta (Deshayes) [Basement Bed], [**18**, 1]
Sigatica hantoniensis (Pilkington), **19**, 18
Siphonalia subnodosa (Morris) [Basement Bed], [**22**, 2, 3]
Solariaxis pulcher (J. de C. Sowerby), **17**, 7
Streptolathyrus cymatodis (Edwards), **24**, 3
Streptolathyrus zonulatus Wrigley, **24**, 1
Surculites errans (Solander), **24**, 10
Tibia lucida (J. Sowerby), **20**, 3, 4
Tornatellaea simulata (Solander), [**27**, 5]
Turricula teretrium (Edwards), **26**, 11
Turritella (Ispharina) sulcifera Deshayes, [**19**, 12]
Xenophora extensa (J. Sowerby), **17**, 15

Cephalopoda   *Belosaepia sepioidea* (Blainville), [**28**, 7]
Cimomia imperialis (J. Sowerby), **28**, 12

Arthropoda   *Arcoscalpellum quadratum* (J. de C. Sowerby), **4**, 1–4
Dromilites lamarcki (Desmarest), **4**, 11
Hoploparia gammaroides McCoy, **4**, 12
Glyphithyreus wetherelli (Bell) **4**, 13
Xanthilites bowerbanki Bell, **4**, 10
Xanthopsis leachi (Desmarest), **4**, 6

Pisces   *Acipenser* sp., [**29**, 4]
Aetobatus irregularis Agassiz [**29**, 1]
Albula eppsi White & Frost [Basement Bed], [**30**, 4]
Cylindracanthus rectus (Dixon), [**30**, 6]
Edaphodon bucklandi Agassiz, [**30**, 2]

Galeorhinus minor (Agassiz), **[28**, 4]
Lamna obliqua (Agassiz), **28**, 1
Notidanus serratissimus Agassiz, **28**, 9
Odontaspis (*Synodontaspis*) *teretidens* White [Basement
                                              Bed], **[28**, 2]
Striatolamia striata (Winkler) [Basement Bed], **[28**, 3]
Phyllodus toliapicus Agassiz, **[30**, 1]
Squatina prima (Winkler), **[28** 10]

Reptilia   *Palaeophis toliapicus* Owen, **30**, 7

LOWER BAGSHOT BEDS (ALUM BAY PLANT BED)

Plantae   *Aralia* sp., **1**, 19
                 Eomastixia rugosa (Zenker), **[1**, 12]

BRACKLESHAM BEDS

(Including Bournemouth Freshwater & Marine Beds, Boscombe Sands)

Plantae   *Brasenia ovula* (Brongniart), **[1**, 6]
                 Eomastixia rugosa (Zenker), **[1**, 12]
                 Limnocarpus forbesi (Heer), **[1**, 17]
                 Nipa burtini (Brongniart), **[1**, 18]
                 Wetherellia variablis Bowerbank, **[1**, 7, 8]

Protozoa   *Alveolina fusiformis* J. de C. Sowerby, **2**, 6
                 Nummulites laevigatus (Brugière), **2**, 4, 5
                 Nummulites variolarius (Lamarck), **2**, 1

Coelenterata *Goniopora websteri* (Bowerbank), **3**, 10
                 Turbinolia dixoni Edwards & Haime, **2**, 9

Annelida   *Protula extensa* (Solander), **[3**, 6]
                 Sclerostyla mellevillei (Nyst & le Hon), **[2**, 7, 8]

Brachiopoda   *Lingula tenuis* J. Sowerby, **[3**, 4]

Bivalvia   *Amusium* (*Lentipecten*) *corneum* (J. Sowerby), **7**, 5
                 Arca biangula Lamarck, **6**, 10
                 Callista (*Microcallista*) *proxima* (Deshayes), **[13**, 4–6]

Cardita (*Venericor*) *planicosta* (Lamarck), **10**, 9, 10
Cardita (*Venericor*) *planicosta suessoniensis* (d'Archiac),
9, 15
Cardium (*Orthocardium*) *porulosum* Solander, [**12**, 13]
Chlamys recondita (Solander), [**7**, 2]
Corbula pisum J. Sowerby, [**14**, 10]
Corbula plicata Wrigley, **14**, 7–9
Corbula (*Bicorbula*) *gallica* Lamarck, **14**, 16–18
Costacallista laevigata (Lamarck), **12**, 1–3
Crassatella compressa Lamarck, **9**, 9, 10
Crassatella sowerbyi S. V. Wood, **9**, 16
Crassatella (*Salaputium*) *aequalis* S. V. Wood, [**9**, 5]
Cultellus affinis (J. Sowerby), [**14**, 2]
Glans oblonga (J. Sowerby), [**9**, 6]
Glycymeris deleta (Solander), [**6**, 8, 9]
Macrosolen hollowaysi (J. Sowerby), **15**, 6–8
Musculus elegans (J. Sowerby), [**6**, 3, 4]
Ostrea plicata Solander, [**9**, 1]
Ostrea tenera J. Sowerby, [**8**, 3]
Panopea intermedia (J. Sowerby), [**16**, 5]
Pitar (*Calpitaria*) *sulcatarius* (Deshayes), [**13**, 1–3]
Psammotaea compressa (J. de C. Sowerby), [**15**, 2–4]
Pteria media (J. Sowerby), [**6**, 7]

Gastropoda   *Ampullonatica ambulacrum* (J. Sowerby), [**18**, 4]
Ancilla canalifera Lamarck, [**16**, 1]
Athleta selseiensis (Edwards), **25**, 4
Athleta (*Volutospina*) *athleta* (Solander), [**26**, 18]
Athleta (*Volutospina*) *nodosus* (J. de C. Sowerby), [**25**, 7]
Athleta (*Volutospina*) *spinosus* (Linné), **25**, 2
Calyptraea aperta (Solander), [**17**, 10]
Campanile cornucopiae (J. Sowerby), **21**, 5
Clavilithes longaevus (Solander), [**23**, 10]
Clavilithes macrospira Cossman, [**23**, 5, 6]
Conomitra parva (J. de C. Sowerby), [**25**, 6]
Cornulina minax (Solander) [**24**, 13]
Crommium willemeti (Deshayes), **18**, 10
Ectinochilus planum (Beyrich), **20**, 9
Epitonium (*Acrilla*) *reticulatum*, (Solander) [**17**, 6]
Euthriofusus regularis (J. Sowerby), [**24**, 11]
Ficus nexilis (Solander), [**21**, 1]

Galeodea coronata (Deshayes), **22**, 7
Globularia grossa (Deshayes), [**18**, 7]
Globularia patula (Lamarck), [**18**, 8]
Globularia sigaretina (Lamarck), [**18**, 9]
Hastula plicatula (Lamarck), [**26**, 14, 15]
Hemipleurotoma plebeia (J. de C. Sowerby), **27**, 6
Hippochrenes amplus (Solander), [**20**, 10]
Leptoconus edwardsi (Cossmann), **27**, 9
Lyria decora (Beyrich), [**25**, 3]
Marginella (*Stazzania*) *bifidoplicata* Charlesworth, [**26**, 5]
Mesalia sulcata (Lamarck), **19**, 7
Olivella (*Callianax*) *branderi* (J. Sowerby), [**16**, 3]
Pollia labiata (J. de C. Sowerby), [**22**, 6]
Pterynotus tricarinatus (Lamarck), [**23**, 2]
Sassia arguta (Solander), [**22**, 4]
Sigatica hantoniensis (Pilkington), [**19**, 18]
Solariaxis pulcher (J. de C. Sowerby), [**17**, 7]
Strepsidura turgida (Solander), **24**, 7
Surculites errans (Solander), [**24**, 10]
Sveltella microstoma (Charlesworth), [**26**, 6]
Sycostoma pyrus (Solander), [**24**, 5]
Terebellum (*Seraphs*) *sopitum* (Solander), [**20**, 8]
Tornatellaea simulata (Solander), [**27**, 5]
Turritella edita (Solander), [**19**, 17]
Turritella (*Haustator*) *imbricataria* Lamarck, **19**, 11
Turritella (*Ispharina*) *sulcifera* Deshayes, **19**, 12
Typhis pungens (Solander), [**23**, 3]
Unitas nassaeformis (Wrigley), [**26**, 12]
Xenophora agglutinans (Lamarck), **18**, 11

Scaphopoda   *Antalis striata* (J. Sowerby), [**28**, 11]

Cephalopoda *Belosaepia sepioidea* (Blainville), **28**, 7

Pisces   *Aetobatus irregularis* Agassiz, **29**, 1
                 Procarcharodon *auriculatus* (Blainville), **28**, 8
                 Cylindracanthus rectus (Dixon), **30**, 6
                 Edaphodon bucklandi Agassiz, **30**, 2
                 Galeocerdo latidens Agassiz, **28**, 6
                 Galeorhinus minor (Agassiz), [**28**, 4]
                 Myliobatis striatus Buckland, [**29**, 2]

Physodon secundus (Winkler), **28**, 5
Squatina prima (Winkler), [**28**, 10]

BARTON BEDS
(INCLUDING HENGISTBURY BEDS)

Plantae   *Brasenia ovula* (Brongniart), [**1**, 6]
Eomastixia rugosa (Zenker), [**1**, 12]
Limnocarpus forbesi (Heer), [**1**, 17]

Protozoa   *Nummulites prestwichianus* (Jones), **2**, 2

Echinoderma   *Ophiura wetherelli* Forbes, [**4**, 7]

Annelida   *Protula extensa* (Solander), **3**, 6
Sclerostyla mellevillei (Nyst & le Hon), **2**, 7, 8

Bivalvia   *Amusium* (*Lentipecten*) *corneum* (J. Sowerby), [**7**, 5]
Arca biangula Lamarck, [**6**, 10]
Callista (*Microcallista*) *heberti belgica* Vincent, **13**, 7, 8
Cardita sulcata (Solander), **9**, 7, 8
Cardita (*Venericor*) *planicosta* (Lamarck), [**10**, 9, 10]
Cardium (*Orthocardium*) *porulosum* Solander, **12**, 13
Chama squamosa Solander, **11**, 2, 3
Chlamys recondita (Solander), **7**, 2
Corbula cuspidata J. Sowerby, [**14**, 14]
Corbula ficus (Solander), **14**, 15
Corbula pisum J. Sowerby, [**14**, 10]
Costacallista laevigata (Lamarck), [**12**, 1–3]
Crassatella sulcata (Solander), **9**, 11, 12
Crassatella (*Salaputium*) *aequalis* S. V. Wood, **9**, 5
Cultellus affinis (J. Sowerby), [**14**, 2]
Erodona plana (J. Sowerby), [**14**, 3–5]
Garum rude (Lamarck), [**15**, 9, 10]
Glans oblonga (J. Sowerby), **9**, 6
Glycymeris deleta (Solander), **6**, 8, 9
Lentidium tawneyi Curry, **14**, 1
Limopsis scalaris (J. de C. Sowerby), **6**, 5, 6
Musculus elegans (J. Sowerby), [**6**, 3, 4]
Nemocardium turgidum (Solander), **12**, 4, 5
Nucula similis J. Sowerby, **5**, 1, 2

Ostrea plicata Solander, **9,** 1
Panopea intermedia (J. Sowerby), [**16,** 5]
Pitar (*Calpitaria*) *sulcatarius* (Deshayes), [**13,** 1–3]
Psammotaea compressa (J. de C. Sowerby), **15,** 2–4
Pteria media (J. Sowerby), [**6,** 7]
Sinodia (*Cordiopsis*) *suborbicularis* (Goldfuss), [**12,** 6–8]
Trinacria curvirostris Cossmann, [**5,** 7, 88]

Gastropoda   *Ampullonatica ambulacrum* (J. Sowerby), **18,** 4
Ancilla canalifera Lamarck, **26,** 1
Architectonica bonneti (Cossmann), **17,** 11
Athleta (*Volutospina*) *athleta* (Solander), **26,** 18
Athleta (*Volutospina*) *luctator* (Solander), **25,** 8–10
Athleta (*Volutospina*) *nodosus* (J. de C. Sowerby), [**25,** 7]
Athleta (*Volutospina*) *scalaris* (J. de C. Sowerby), **25,** 1
Athleta (*Volutospina*) *spinosus* (Linné), [**25,** 2]
Bartonia canaliculata (J. de C. Sowerby), **23,** 9
Bathytoma turbida (Solander), **26,** 16, 17
Batillaria concava (J. Sowerby), [**19,** 10]
Bonellitia evulsa (Solander), **26,** 7
Calliostoma nodulosum (Solander), **17,** 1
Calyptraea aperta (Solander), **17,** 10
Clavilithes longaevus (Solander), **23,** 10
Clavilithes macrospira Cossmann, **23,** 5, 6
Conomitra parva (J. de C. Sowerby), **25,** 6
Conorbis dormitor (Solander), **26,** 2
Coptostoma quadratum (J. Sowerby), **26,** 9
Cornulina minax (Solander), **24,** 13
Dientomochilus bartonense (J. Sowerby), **20,** 7
Ectinochilus planum (Beyrich), [**20,** 9]
Epitonium (*Acrilla*) *reticulatum* (Solander), **17,** 6
Euspira bartonensis Wrigley, **18,** 3
Euthriofusus regularis (J. Sowerby), **24,** 11
Ficus nexilis (Solander), **21,** 1
Fusinus asper (J. Sowerby), **23,** 8
Fusinus porrectus (Solander), **23,** 11
Globularia grossa (Deshayes), **17,** 7
Globularia patula (Lamarck), **18,** 8
Globularia sigaretina (Lamarck), **18,** 9
Hastula plicatula (Lamarck), [**26,** 14, 15]
Hemiconus scabriculus (Solander), **27,** 10

Hemipleurotoma plebia (J. de C. Sowerby), [27, 6]
Hippochrenes amplus (Solander), **20**, 10
Lyria decora (Beyrich) [**25**, 3]
Marginella (*Stazzania*) *bifidoplicata* Charlesworth, **26**, 5
Melanella (*Polygireulima*) *polygyra* (Charlesworth), **17**, 9
Mitreola scabra (J. de C. Sowerby), **26**, 8
Olivella (*Callianax*) *branderi* (J. Sowerby), **26**, 3
Pterynotus tricarinatus (Lamarck), **23**, 2
Rimella rimosa (Solander), **20**, 2
Rostreulima macrostroma (Charlesworth), **17**, 5
Sassia arguta (Solander), **22**, 4
Sconsia ambigua (Solander), **22**, 5
Sigatica hantoniensis (Pilkington), [**19**, 18]
Strepsidura turgida (Solander), [**24**, 7]
Surculites errans (Solander), [**24**, 10]
Sveltella microstoma (Charlesworth), **26**, 6
Sycostoma pyrus (Solander), **24**, 5
Terebellum (*Seraphs*) *sopitum* (Solander), **20**, 8
Tornatellaea simulata (Solander), **27**, 5
Turricula rostrata (Solander), **26**, 10
Turritella edita (Solander), **19**, 17
Turritella (*Haustator*) *imbricataria* Lamarck, [**19**, 11]
Typhis pungens (Solander), **23**, 3
Unitas nassaeformis (Wrigley), **26**, 12
Urosalpinx sexdentatus (J. de C. Sowerby), [**23**, 7]
Volutocorbis ambigua (Solander), **24**, 12
Volutocorbis scabricula (Solander), **24**, 8
Xenophora agglutinans (Lamarck), [**18**, 11]

Scaphopoda   "*Antalis striata*" (J. Sowerby), **28**, 11

Cephalopoda   *Belosaepia sepioidea* (Blainville), [**28**, 7]

Pisces   *Aetobatus irregularis* Agassiz, [**29**, 1]
Procarcharodon auriculatus (Blainville), [**28**, 8]
Cylindracanthus rectus (Dixon), [**30**, 6]
Eugaleus minor (Agassiz), **28**, 4
Galeocerdo latidens Agassiz, [**28**, 6]
Myliobatis striatus Buckland, **20**, 2
Physodon secundus (Winkler), [**28**, 5]
Squatina prima (Winkler), [**28**, 10]

EOCENE and OLIGOCENE

HEADON BEDS

Plantae
Brasenia ovula (Brongniart), **1**, 6
Chara medicaginula (Lamarck), **1**, 11
Eomastixia rugosa (Zenker), **1**, 12
Limnocarpus forbesi (Heer), **1**, 17

Bivalvia
Arca biangula Lamarck [Brockenhurst Bed], [**6**, 10]
Arctica planata (J. de C. Sowerby) [Brockenhurst Bed],
[**11**, 7]
Cardita deltoidea (J. Sowerby), **9**, 13, 14
Cardium (*Orthocardium*) *porulosum* Solander, **12**, 13
Corbicula obovata (J. Sowerby), **11**, 1
Corbula cuspidata J. Sowerby, **14**, 14
Corbula pisum J. Sowerby, [**14**, 10]
Costacallista laevigata (Lamarck), [**12**, 1–3]
Erodona plana (J. Sowerby), **14**, 3–5
Garum rude (Lamarck), **15**, 9, 10
Lentidium tawneyi Curry, [**14**, 1]
Musculus elegans (J. Sowerby), [**6**, 3, 4]
Ostrea plicata Solander, [**9**, 1]
Ostrea velata S. V. Wood, **8**, 1, 2
Panopea intermedia (J. Sowerby), [**16**, 5]
Psammotaea compressa (J. de C. Sowerby), [**15**, 2–4]
Pteria media (J. Sowerby), [**6**, 7]
Sinodia (*Cordiopsis*) *suborbicularis* (Goldfuss), **12**, 6–8
Trinacria curvirostris Cossmann, **5**, 7, 8

Gastropoda
Athleta (*Volutospina*) *spinosus* (Linné), [**25**, 2]
Batillaria concava (J. Sowerby), **19**, 10
Batillaria ventricosa (J. Sowerby), **19**, 15, 16
Bonellitia pyrgota (Edwards), **26**, 13
Calyptraea aperta (Solander), [**17**, 10]
Cornulina minax (Solander), [**24**, 13]
Filholia elliptica (J. Sowerby), [**27**, 11]
Galba longiscata (Brongniart), **27**, 7
Globularia grossa (Deshayes), [**18**, 7]
Hemipleurotoma plebeia (J. de C. Sowerby), [**27**, 6]
Lyria decora (Beyrich), **25**, 3
Melanoides (*Tarebia*) *acuta* (J. Sowerby), **19**, 2

Planorbina discus (Edwards), [27, 4]
Planorbina euomphalus (J. Sowerby), **27**, 8
Pollia labiata (J. de C. Sowerby), **22**, 6
Potamaclis turritissima (Forbes), [**19**, 9]
Potamides (*Ptychopotamides*) *vagus* (Solander), **19**, 3, 4
Pterynotus hantoniensis (Edwards), **23**, 4
Rimella rimosa (Solander), [**20**, 2]
Sconsia ambigua (Solander), [**22**, 5]
Sigatica hantoniensis (Pilkington), [**19**, 18]
Terebellum (*Seraphs*) *sopitum* (Solander), [**20**, 8]
Theodoxus apertus (J. de C. Sowerby), **17**, 2, 3
Theodoxus concavus (J. de C. Sowerby), **17**, 4
Typhis pungens (Solander), [**23**, 3]
Urosalpinx sexdentatus (J. de C. Sowerby), **23**, 7
Viviparus angulosus (J. Sowerby), [**17**, 13]
Viviparus lentus (Solander), **17**, 14

Pisces   *Acipenser* sp., [**28**, 4]
          Amia sp., [**30**, 3]

Reptilia   *Diplocynodon hantoniensis* (Wood), **30**, 8, 9
           Trionyx circumsulcatus Owen, **30**, 10

OLIGOCENE
OSBORNE BEDS

Plantae   *Chara medicaginula* (Lamarck), [**1**, 11]

Gastropoda   *Filholia elliptica* (J. Sowerby), [**27**, 11]
             Galba longiscata (Brongniart), [**27**, 7]
             Melanoides (*Tarebia*) *acuta* (J. Sowerby), [**19**, 2]
             Viviparus angulosus (J. Sowerby), [**17**, 13]
             Viviparus lentus (Solander), [**17**, 14]

Pisces   *Amia* sp., [**30**, 3]

Mammalia   *Plagiolophus minor* (Cuvier), [**30**, 11]

BEMBRIDGE BEDS

Plantae   *Brasenia ovula* (Brongniart), [**1**, 6]
          Chara medicaginula (Lamarck), [**1**, 11]
          Limnocarpus forbesi (Heer), [**1**, 17]

Bivalvia   *Polymesoda convexa* (Brongniart), **[10,** 1–3]
                  Sinodia (*Cordiopsis*) *suborbicularis* (Goldfuss), **[12,** 6–8]
                  Trinacria curvirostris Cossmann **[5,** 7, 8]

Gastropoda   *Filholia elliptica* (J. Sowerby), **27,** 11
                  Galba longiscata (Brongniart), **[27,** 7]
                  Klikia vectiensis (Edwards), **27,** 3
                  Megalocochlea pseudoglobosa (d'Orbigny), **27,** 2
                  Melanoides (*Tarebia*) *acuta* (J. Sowerby), **[19,** 2]
                  Palaeoglandina costellata (J. Sowerby), **27,** 12
                  Palaeoxestina occlusa (Edwards), **27,** 1
                  Planorbina discus (Edwards), **27,** 4
                  Potamaclis turritissima (Forbes), **[19,** 9]
                  Viviparus angulosus (J. Sowerby), **17,** 13
                  Viviparus lentus (Solander) **[17,** 14]

Pisces   *Amia* sp., **30,** 3

Mammalia   *Plagiolophus minor* (Cuvier), **30,** 11

                         HAMSTEAD BEDS

Plantae   *Brasenia ovula* (Brongniart), **[1,** 6]
                  Chara medicaginula (Lamarck), **[1,** 11]
                  Limnocarpus forbesi (Heer), **[1,** 17]
                  Stratiotes websteri (Brongniart), **[1,** 9]

Bivalvia   *Polymesoda convexa* (Brongniart), **10,** 1–3

Gastropoda   *Athleta* (*Neoathleta*) *rathieri* (Hébert), **24,** 9
                  Melanoides (*Tarebia*) *acuta* (J. Sowerby), **[19,** 2]
                  Nystia duchasteli (Nyst), **17,** 12
                  Pirenella monilifera (Defrance), **19,** 6
                  Planorbina discus (Edwards), **[27,** 4]
                  Potamaclis turritissima (Forbes), **19,** 9
                  Viviparus lentus (Solander), **[17,** 14]
                  Theodoxus concavus (J. de C. Sowerby), **[17, 4]**

Pisces   *Acipenser* sp., **29,** 4
                  Amia sp., **[30,** 3]

BOVEY TRACEY BEDS

Plantae   *Stratiotes websteri* (Brongniart), **1, 9**

PLIOCENE
CORALLINE CRAG

Coelenterata   *Sphenotrochus intermedius* (Münster), **21**, 2

Echinoderma   *Temnechinus excavatus* Forbes, **32**, 4

Polyzoa   *Meandropora tubipora* (Busk), **31**, 1

Brachiopoda   *Terebratula maxima* Charlesworth, **32**, 3

Bivalvia   *Arctica islandica* (Linné), **35**, 4, 5
Astarte mutabilis S. V. Wood, **35**, 6
Astarte omalii de la Jonkaire, [**35**, 3]
Cardita senilis (Lamarck), **35**, 1
Cardium (*Cerastoderma*) *edule* Linné, [**36**, 3]
Chlamys (*Aequipecten*) *opercularis* (Linné), **33**, 7, 8
Chlamys (*Palliolum*) *tigerina* (Müller), **33**, 4, 5
Cyclocardia scalaris (J. Sowerby), [**35**, 2]
Digitaria digitaria (Linné), [**35**, 7]
Glycymeris glycymeris (Linné), [**33**, 6]
Macoma obliqua (J. Sowerby), **38**, 7–9
Mya truncata (Linné), **38**, 10, 11
Ostrea edulis Linné, **34**, 7, 8
Phacoides (*Lucinoma*) *borealis* (Linné) **36**, 5–7
Pseudamussium gerardi (Nyst), **34**, 1, 2,
Pteromeris corbis (Philippi), **35**, 8
Spisula arcuata (J. Sowerby), [**27**, 5]
Venus casina Linné, [**36**, 8, 9]

Gastropoda   *Admete viridula* (Fabricius), [**41**, 8]
Calliostoma subexcavatum (S. V. Wood), [**39, 1**]
Calyptraea chinensis (Linné), **39**, 9
Capulus ungaricus (Linné), [**39**, 12]
Emarginula reticulata J. Sowerby, [**39**, 2]
Hinia reticosa (J. Sowerby), [**40**, 1]
Hinia granulata (J. Sowerby), [**29**, 4]

Leiomesus dalei (J. Sowerby), [**40**, 4]
Lunatia catenoides (S. V. Wood), [**39**, 15]
Natica multipunctata S. V. Wood [**39**, 13]
Nucella tetragona (J. Sowerby), [**40**, 8]
Potamides tricinctus (Brocchi), [**39**, 7, 8]
Ringicula ventricosa (J. de C. Sowerby), [**41**, 14]
Scaphella lamberti (J. Sowerby), [**41**, 5]
Searlesia costifera (S. V. Wood), [**40**, 6]
Trivia coccinelloides (J. Sowerby), [**39**, 10]
Trophonopsis (*Boreotrophon*) *clathratus* (Linné), [**40**, 3]
Turritella (*Haustator*) *incrassata* J. Sowerby, **39**, 5

Arthropoda   *Balanus concavus* Bronn, **32**, 2

Pisces   *Isurus hastalis* (Agassiz), [**41**, 3]
Raja clavata Linné, [**41**, 2]

PLEISTOCENE
RED CRAG

Coelenterata   *Balanophyllia caliculus* S. V. Wood, **31**, 4
Sphenotrochus intermedius (Münster), [**31**, 2]

Echinoderma   *Echinocyamus pusillus* (Müller), **31**, 3

Bivalvia   *Acila cobboldiae* (J. Sowerby), **33**, 3
Arctica islandica (Linné), [**35**, 4, 5]
Astarte mutabilis S. V. Wood, [**35**, 6]
Astarte obliquata J. Sowerby, **34**, 3, 4
Astarte omalii de la Jonkaire, **35**, 3
Cardita senilis (Lamarck), [**35**, 1]
Cardium (*Acanthocardium*) *parkinsoni* J. Sowerby, **36**, 1, 2
Cardium (*Cerastoderma*) *angustatum* J. Sowerby, **36**, 4
Cardium (*Cerastoderma*) *edule* Linné, **36**, 3
Chlamys (*Aequipecten*) *opercularis* (Linné), [**33**, 7, 8]
Chlamys (*Palliolum*) *tigerina* (Müller), [**33**, 4, 5]
Cyclocardia scalaris (J. Sowerby), **35**, 2
Digitaria digitaria (Linné), **35**, 7
Dosinia exoleta (Linné), **37**, 1–3
Glycymeris glycymeris (Linné), **33**, 6

Macoma calcarea (Gmelin), [**38**, 2]
Macoma obliqua (J. Sowerby), **38**, 7–9
Macoma praetenuis (Woodward), **38**, 1
Mya truncata (Linné), [**38**, 10, 11]
Mytilus edulis Linné, **34**, 6
Nucula laevigata J. Sowerby, **33**, 1, 2
Ostrea edulis Linné, [**34**, 7, 8]
Phacoides (*Lucinoma*) *borealis* (Linné), [**36**, 5–7]
Pteromeris corbis (Phillippi), [**35**, 8]
Scrobicularia plana (Da Costa), [**37**, 4]
Spisula arcuata (J. Sowerby), **37**, 5
Venus casina Linné, **36**, 8, 9
Yoldia oblongoides (S. V. Wood), [**32**, 1]

Gastropoda

Admete viridula (Fabricius), **41**, 8
Buccinum undatum Linné, [**40**, 2]
Calliostoma subexcavatum (S. V. Wood), **39**, 1
Calyptraea chinensis (Linné), [**39**, 9]
Capulus ungaricus (Linné), **39**, 12
Emarginula reticulata J. Sowerby, **29**, 2
Epitonium (*Boreoscala*) *greenlandicum* (Perry), [**39**, 3]
Helix (*Cepaea*) *nemoralis* Linné, **42**, 4
Hinia granulata (J. Sowerby), **39**, 4
Hinia reticosa (J. Sowerby), **40**, 1
Hygromia (*Trichia*) *hispida* (Linné), [**42**, 2]
Leiomesus dalei (J. Sowerby), **40**, 4
Littorina littorea (Linné), **39**, 14
Lunatia catenoides (S. V. Wood), **39**, 15
Lymnaea (*Radix*) *peregra* (Müller), [**41**, 9]
Natica multipunctata S. V. Wood **39**, 13
Neptunea contraria (Linné), **40**, 7
Neptunea despecta decemcostata (Say), **40**, 5
Nucella incrassata (J. Sowerby), **41**, 1
Nucella tetragona (J. Sowerby), **40**, 8
Polinices hemiclausus (J. Sowerby), **39**, 11
Potamides tricinctus (Brocchi), **39**, 7, 8
Pupilla muscorum (Linné), [**42**, 3]
Ringicula ventricosa (J. de C. Sowerby), **41**, 14
Scaphella lamberti (J. Sowerby), **41**, 5
Searlesia costifera (S. V. Wood), **40**, 6
Sipho curtus (Jeffreys), **40**, 9

24 *British Caenozoic Fossils*

Trivia coccinelloides (J. Sowerby), **39**, 10
Trophonopsis (*Boreotrophon*) *clathratus* (Linné), [**40**, 3]
Turritella (*Haustator*) *incrassata* J. Sowerby, [**39**, 5]

Arthropoda   *Balanus concavus* Bronn, [**32**, 2]

Pisces   *Acipenser* sp., [**29**, 4]
Isurus hastalis (Agassiz), **41**, 3
Raja clavata Linné [in Nodule Bed], [**41**, 2]

Mammalia   *Balaena affinis* Owen, **41**, 4
Anancus arvernensis (Croizet & Jobert), **44**, 2

NORWICH CRAG

Echinoderma   *Echinocyamus pusillus* (Müller), [**31**, 3]

Bivalvia   *Acila cobboldiae* (J. Sowerby), [**33**, 3]
Arctica islandica (Linné), [**35**, 4, 5]
Astarte semisulcata (Leach), [**34**, 5]
Cardium (*Cerastoderma*) *angustatum* J. Sowerby, [**36**, 4]
Cardium (*Cerastoderma*) *edule* Linné, [**36**, 3]
Chlamys (*Aequipecten*) *opercularis* (Linné), [**33**, 7, 8]
Corbicula fluminalis (Müller), [**42**, 8, 9]
Glycymeris glycymeris (Linné), [**33**, 6]
Macoma calcarea (Gmelin), [**38**, 2]
Macoma obliqua (J. Sowerby), [**38**, 7–9]
Macoma praetenuis (Woodward), [**38**, 1]
Mya truncata (Linné), [**38**, 10, 11]
Mytilus edulis Linné, [**34**, 6]
Ostrea edulis Linné [**34**, 7, 8]
Phacoides (*Lucinoma*) *borealis* (Linné), [**36**, 5–7]
Pisidium clessini Neumayr, [**42**, 7]
Scrobicularia plana (Da Costa), [**37**, 4]
Spisula arcuata (J. Sowerby), [**37**, 5]
Spisula subtruncata (Da Costa), **38**, 3
Yoldia oblongoides (S. V. Wood), **32**, 1

Gastropoda   *Admete viridula* (Fabricius), [**41**, 8]
Bithynia tentaculata (Linné), [**41**, 11, 12]
Buccinum undatum Linné, [**40**, 2]

Calyptraea chinensis (Linné), [**39**, 8]
Capulus ungaricus (Linné), [**39**, 12]
Epitonium (*Boreoscala*) *greenlandicum* (Perry), **39**, 3
Hygromia (*Trichia*) *hispida* (Linné), [**42**, 2]
Leiomesus dalei (J. Sowerby), [**40**, 4]
Littorina littorea (Linné), [**39**, 14]
Lymnaea (*Radix*) *peregra* (Müller), [**41**, 9]
Neptunea contraria (Linné), [**40**, 7]
Neptunea despecta decemcostata (Say), [**40**, 5]
Nucella incrassata (J. Sowerby), [**41**, 1]
Polinices hemiclausus (J. Sowerby), [**39**, 11]
Potamides tricinctus (Brocchi), **39**, 7, 8
Pupilla muscorum (Linné), [**42**, 3]
Ringicula ventricosa (J. de C. Sowerby), [**41**, 14]
Succinea oblonga Draparnaud, [**42**, 1]
Trophonopsis (*Boreotrophon*) *clathratus* (Linné), [**40**, 3]
Turritella (*Haustator*) *incrassata* J. Sowerby, [**39**, 5]

Pisces   *Raja clavata* Linné, **41**, 2

Mammalia   *Anancus arvernensis* (Croizet & Jobert) [**44**, 2]
                 Palaeoloxodon antiquus (Falconer & Cautley), [**44**, 3]

CHILLESFORD BEDS

Echinoderma *Echinocyamus pusillus* (Müller), [**31**, 3]

Bivalvia   *Acila cobboldiae* (J. Sowerby), [**33**, 3]
                 Arctica islandica (Linné), [**35**, 4, 5]
                 Astarte semisulcata (Leach), [**34**, 5]
                 Cardium (*Cerastoderma*) *edule* Linné, [**36**, 3]
                 Chlamys (*Aequipecten*) *opercularis* (Linné), [**33**, 8, 7]
                 Chlamys (*Palliolum*) *tigerina* (Müller), [**33**, 3, 5]
                 Corbicula fluminalis (Müller), [**42** 8, 9]
                 Glycymeris glycymeris (Linné), [**33**, 6]
                 Macoma calcarea (Gmelin), **38**, 2
                 Macoma obliqua (J. Sowerby), [**38**, 7–9]
                 Macoma praetenuis (Woodward), [**28**, 11]
                 Mya truncata (Linné), [**38**, 10, 11]
                 Mytilis edulis Linné, [**34**, 6]
                 Phacoides (*Lucinoma*) *borealis* (Linné), [**36**, 5–7]

Pisidium clessini Neumayr, [42, 7]
Pteromeris corbis (Philippi), [35, 8]
Scrobicularia plana (Da Costa), [37, 4]
Spisula arcuata (J. Sowerby), [37, 5]
Spisula subtruncata (Da Costa), [38, 3]
Yoldia oblongoides (S. V. Wood), [32, 1]

Gastropoda
Buccinum undatum Linné, [40, 2]
Calyptraea chinensis (Linné), [39, 9]
Epitonium (*Boreoscala*) *greenlandicum* (Perry), [38, 3]
Hinia reticosa (J. Sowerby), [40, 1]
Hygromia (*Trichia*) *hispida* (Linné), [42, 2]
Leiomesus dalei (J. Sowerby), [40, 4]
Littorina littorea (Linné), [39, 14]
Lymnaea (*Radix*) *peregra* (Müller), [41, 9]
Neptunea contraria (Linné), [40, 7]
Nucella incrassata (J. Sowerby), [41, 1]
Polinices hemiclausus (J. Sowerby), [39, 11]
Potamides tricinctus (Brocchi), [39, 7, 8]

WEYBOURNE CRAG

Bivalvia
Acila cobboldiae (J. Sowerby), [33, 3]
Arctica islandica (Linné), [35, 4, 5]
Astarte semisulcata (Leach), [34, 5]
Cardium (*Cerastoderma*) *edule* Linné, [36, 3]
Corbicula fluminalis (Müller), [42, 8, 9]
Macoma balthica (Linné), [38, 5–6]
Macoma calcarea (Gmelin), [38, 2]
Macoma obliqua (J. Sowerby), [38, 7–9]
Mya truncata (Linné), [38, 10, 11]
Mytilus edulis (Linné), [34, 6]
Phacoides (*Lucinoma*) *borealis* (Linné), [36, 5–7]
Pisidium clessini Neumayr, [42, 7]
Scrobicularia plana (Da Costa), [37, 4]
Yoldia oblongoides (S. V. Wood,) [32, 1]

Gastropoda
Admete viridula (Fabricius), [41, 8]
Buccinum undatum Linné, [40, 2]
Epitonium (*Boreoscala*) *greenlandicum* (Perry), [39, 3]

Hygromia (*Trichia*) *hispida* (Linné), [**42**, 2]
Littorina littorea (Linné), [**39**, 14]
Neptunea contraria (Linné), [**40**, 7]
Nucella incrassata (J. Sowerby), [**41**, 1]
Polinices hemiclausus (J. Sowerby), [**39**, 11]
Succinea oblonga Draparnaud, [**42**, 1]
Trophonopsis (*Boreotrophon*) *clathratus* (Linné), [**40**, 3]

Pisces   *Raja clavata* Linné, [**41**, 2]

NEW ARRIVALS IN BRITAIN AFTER THE WEYBOURNE CRAG

Bivalvia   *Unio* (*Potomida*) *littoralis* Cuvier, **42**, 5, 6

Gastropoda   *Ancylus fluviatilis* Müller, **41**, 6
Belgrandia marginata (Michaud), **41**, 7
Planorbis planorbis (Linné), **41**, 15
Turritella communis Risso, **39**, 6
† *Valvata antiqua* Morris, **41**, 10
† *Viviparus diluvianus* (Kunth), **41**, 13

Mammalia   † *Bos primigenius* Bojanus, **43**, 3, 4
Cervus elaphus Linné, **42**, 8
† *Coelodonta antiquitatis* (Blumenbach), **43**, 5
† *Crocuta crocuta spelaea* Goldfuss, **44**, 4
† *Dama clactoniana* (Falconer), **43**, 10
Hippopotamus amphibius Linné, **43**, 6
† *Mammuthus primigenius* (Blumenbach), **44**, 1
† *Megaceros giganteus* (Blumenbach), **43**, 9
Rangifer tarandus (Linné), **43**, 7
† *Ursus deningeri* von Reichenau, **44**, 5

          † Race or species now extinct

GEOLOGICAL TIME-SCALE†

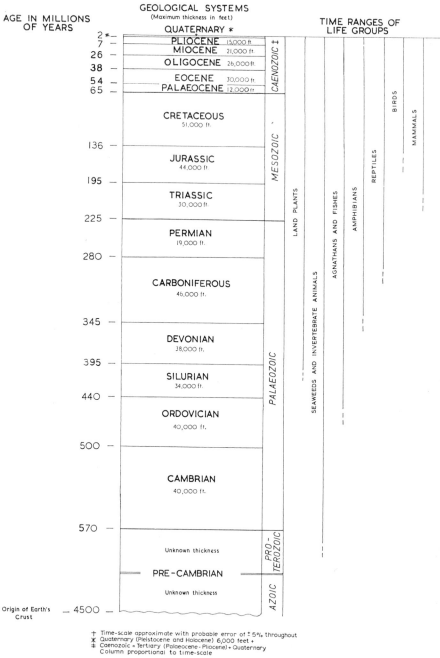

GEOLOGICAL SYSTEMS
(Maximum thickness in feet)

AGE IN MILLIONS
OF YEARS

TIME RANGES OF
LIFE GROUPS

QUATERNARY *

2 *—	PLIOCENE	15,000 ft.	CAENOZOIC ‡
7 —	MIOCENE	21,000 ft.	
26 —	OLIGOCENE	26,000 ft.	
38 —	EOCENE	30,000 ft.	
54 —	PALAEOCENE	12,000 ft.	
65 —			

CRETACEOUS
51,000 ft.

136 —

JURASSIC
44,000 ft.

195 —

TRIASSIC
30,000 ft.

225 —

PERMIAN
19,000 ft.

280 —

CARBONIFEROUS
46,000 ft.

345 —

DEVONIAN
38,000 ft.

395 —

SILURIAN
34,000 ft.

440 —

ORDOVICIAN
40,000 ft.

500 —

CAMBRIAN
40,000 ft.

570 —

PRO-TEROZOIC

Unknown thickness

PRE-CAMBRIAN

AZOIC

Unknown thickness

Origin of Earth's — 4500 —
Crust

MESOZOIC

PALAEOZOIC

BIRDS

MAMMALS

REPTILES

LAND PLANTS

AMPHIBIANS

AGNATHANS AND FISHES

SEAWEEDS AND INVERTEBRATE ANIMALS

† Time-scale approximate with probable error of ± 5% throughout
✗ Quaternary (Pleistocene and Holocene) 6,000 feet +
‡ Caenozoic = Tertiary (Palaeocene - Pliocene) + Quaternary
    Column proportional to time-scale

28

The Scientific Names of Fossils

The scientific name of a species is established by its publication with a description of the distinctive characters and preferably also with an illustration of the species. The worker describing the latter is alluded to as its author. The name of each species consists essentially of two words which are either Latin or treated as Latin. The first word is the name of the genus to which the species is assigned, and the second (the specific name) indicates the species. Sometimes the species of a genus are grouped in subgenera which also have Latin names. The subgeneric name is then placed between the generic and specific names, but in round brackets. The name of the author of a species is usually placed after the specific name; this gives a clue to where the description of a species is to be found. If the species has been transferred to a different genus from that under which it was originally described, its author's name is placed in round brackets. If the specific name is an adjective, it must agree in gender with the generic name. Some specific names, however, are nouns in the genitive or in apposition to the generic name and are not liable to change according to the gender of the latter.

Sometimes it is desired to indicate that a specimen belongs to a definite subspecies, that is, a group in which, perhaps, geographical isolation or evolutionary changes have resulted in slight differences from typical specimens of the species. In such cases a Latin subspecific name is used, and this and its author's name follow the names already mentioned.

The same genus or species has sometimes been described by different workers under different names, and in such cases the name first used must be accepted. The discovery of earlier names has thus been one reason for changes in nomenclature. A more important cause of changes in the names of organisms lies in the fact that nomenclature is dependent upon classification. Increased knowledge of a species may show that it was referred by its author to a genus with which it has no affinity, as in the case of the species from the Thanet Sands which was originally called *Pholadomya cuneata*, but is now known not to belong even to the same family as *Pholadomya* and is placed in the genus *Eutylus*. Moreover, one worker will treat a group of species as a distinct genus, while another will include the same group in a genus described earlier. Similarly, one worker will unite in a single species a series of specimens which another will

29

consider to belong to two or more distinct species. The views of modern authorities have been the main criterion in deciding what name should be used for any species illustrated in the present booklet. Other names which have been used from time to time (and which may differ in either the generic or the specific name, or in both) are, if thought important enough, cited as synonyms (abbreviation, "syn.").

L.R.C.

Explanation of Plates

The range given for each species is that at present known and applies to Great Britain only.

Two or more drawings bearing the same number and usually linked by a broken line are views of the same specimen.

The specific names, quoted in square brackets after the abbreviation Syn. (= Synonym), are other names that have been used, often incorrectly, for the species. (See p. 27.)

*Species exhibited in second bay of Fossil Mammal Gallery.

Plate 1

Eocene and Oligocene Plants

1. **Anonaspermum rotundatum** Reid and Chandler. Seed. (×1.) London Clay, Sheppey, Kent. RANGE: London Clay.

2. **Iodes corniculata** Reid and Chandler. Part of fruit. (×3.) London Clay, Sheppey, Kent. RANGE: London Clay.

3. **Magnolia lobata** (Bowerbank). Internal mould of seed. (×2.) London Clay, Sheppey, Kent. RANGE: London Clay.

4, 5. **Oncoba variabilis** (Bowerbank). (×1.) 4, fruit; 5, segment of fruit with seeds. London Clay, Sheppey, Kent. RANGE: London Clay.

6. **Brasenia ovula** (Brongiart). Seed. (×6.) Lower Headon Beds, Hordle, Hants. RANGE: Bournemouth Marine–Hamstead Beds.

7, 8. **Wetherellia variabilis** Bowerbank. (×1.) 7, fruit; 8, segment of fruit. London Clay, Sheppey, Kent. RANGE: London Clay–Bracklesham Beds.

9.* **Stratiotes websteri** (Brongniart). Water Soldier seed. (×3.) Middle Oligocene lignite, Bovey Tracey, Devon. RANGE: Hamstead and Bovey Tracey Beds.

10. **Cinnamomum globulare** Reid and Chandler. Cinnamon berry. (×1.) London Clay, Sheppey, Kent. RANGE: London Clay.

11. **Chara medicaginula** (Lamarck). Part of the fruit. (×30.) Lower Headon Beds, Hordle, Hants. RANGE: London Clay, Headon–Hamstead Beds.

12. **Eomastixia rugosa** (Zenker). Part of fruit. (×1.) Lower Headon Beds, Hordle, Hants. RANGE: Lower Bagshot–Lower Headon Beds. [Syn., *Eomastixia bilocularis* Chandler.]

13. **Hightea elliptica** Bowerbank. Worn fruit showing two seeds. (×1½.) London Clay, Sheppey, Kent. RANGE: London Clay.

14, 15. **Hightea turgida** Bowerbank. (×1.) 14, columella apex; 15, worn fruit. London Clay, Sheppey, Kent. RANGE: London Clay.

16. **Petrophiloides richardsoni** Bowerbank. Catkin. (×1.) London Clay, Swalecliffe, near Herne Bay, Kent. RANGE: London Clay.

17. **Limnocarpus forbesi** (Heer). Part of fruit. (×10.) Lower Headon Beds, Hordle, Hants. RANGE: Bournemouth Marine–Hamstead Beds. [Syn., *Limnocarpus headonensis* (Gardner).]

18. **Nipa burtini** (Brongniart). Fruit of stemless Palm. (×1.) (After Bowerbank.) London Clay, Sheppey, Kent. RANGE: London Clay –Bournemouth Marine Beds.

19.* **Aralia** sp. Leaf. (×½.) Bagshot Beds, Alum Bay, Isle of Wight. RANGE: Bagshot Beds.

Plate 1

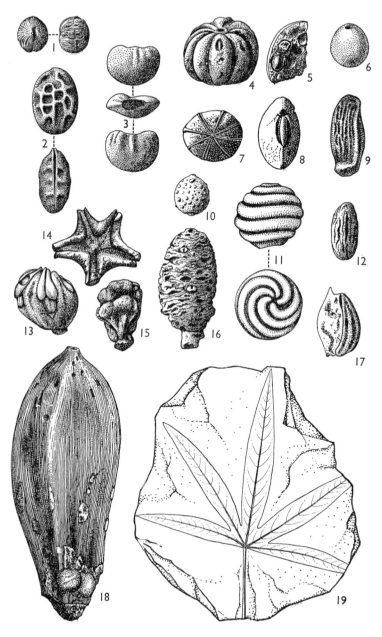

33

Plate 2

Eocene Foraminifera (Figs. 1–6), Worm Tube (Figs. 7, 8) and Corals (Figs. 9, 10)

1. **Nummulites variolarius** (Lamarck). (×15.) Upper Bracklesham Beds, Lee-on-Solent, Hants. RANGE: Upper Bracklesham Beds. (Often wrongly recorded from Barton Beds.)

2. **Nummulites prestwichianus** (Jones). (×10.) Lower Barton Beds, Alum Bay, Isle of Wight. RANGE: Lower Barton Beds. [Syn., *N. elegans* (J. de C. Sowerby), *N. orbignyi* (Galeotti), *N. wemmelensis* de la Harpe and van den Broeck.]

3. **Marginulina wetherelli** Jones. (×15.) London Clay, Piccadilly, London. RANGE: London Clay. [Syn., *M. enbornensis* Bowen.]

4, 5.* **Nummulites laevigatus** (Brugiere). (×3.) 4, part of surface removed to show whorls and septa; 5, vertical section. Lower Bracklesham Beds, Southampton Docks, Hants. RANGE: Lower Bracklesham Beds. [Syn., *N. lamarcki* d'Archiac and Haime.]

6. **Alveolina fusiformis** J. de C. Sowerby. (×5.) Upper Bracklesham Beds, Selsey, Sussex. RANGE: Upper Bracklesham Beds. [Syn., *A. bosci* of authors, *A. sabulosa* (Montfort).]

7, 8. **Sclerostyla mellevillei** (Nyst & le Hon). 7, tube with operculum in place (×1); 8, operculum enlarged (×3). Barton Beds, Barton, Hants. RANGE: Bracklesham–Barton Beds.

9. **Turbinolia dixoni** Edwards & Haime. (×2½.) Bracklesham Beds, Bracklesham Bay, Sussex. RANGE: Bracklesham Beds.

10.* **Goniopora websteri** (Bowerbank). *a* (×1); *b* (×7½). Bracklesham Beds, Bracklesham Bay, Sussex. RANGE: Bracklesham Beds.

Plate 2

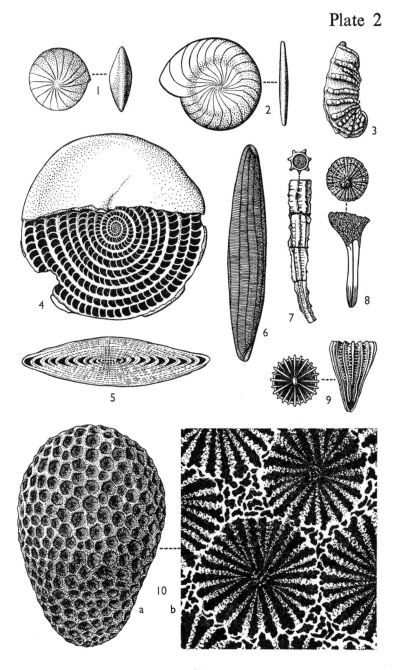

Plate 3

Eocene Brachiopods (Figs. 1–5), Worm Tubes (Figs. 6–8) and Coral (Fig. 9)

1, 2.* **Terebratula hantonensis** Muir-Wood. (1, ×1; 2, interior, ×1½.) London Clay, Catisfield railway cutting, Fareham, Hants. RANGE: London Clay.

3.* **Terebratulina wardenensis** Elliott. (×1¼.) London Clay, Sheppey, Kent. RANGE: London Clay. [Syn., *T. striatula* of authors.]

4. **Lingula tenuis** J. Sowerby. (×2.) London Clay, Bognor Regis, Sussex. RANGE: London Clay–Lower Bracklesham Beds.

5. **Discinisca ferroviae** Muir-Wood. (×3.) Woolwich Beds, Tooting, South London. RANGE: Woolwich–Blackheath Beds.

6.* **Protula extensa** (Solander). (×1.) Middle Barton Beds, Barton, Hants. RANGE: Bracklesham–Barton Beds. [Syn., *Serpula extensa*.]

7.* **Ditrupa plana** (J. Sowerby). (×1.) London Clay, Tolworth, Surrey. RANGE: London Clay.

8.* **Rotularia bognoriensis** (Mantell). (×1.) London Clay, Bognor Regis, Sussex. RANGE: Middle and Upper London Clay. [Syn., *Vermetus bognoriensis*.]

9.* **Paracyathus crassus** Edwards and Haime. (×10.) London Clay, Clarendon, Wilts. RANGE: London Clay.

Plate 3

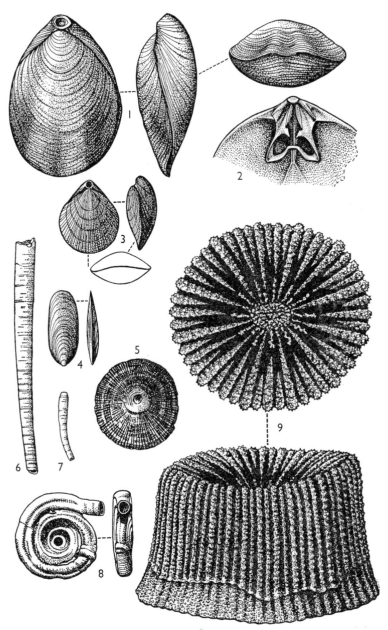

Plate 4

Eocene Arthropods (Figs. 1–4, 6, 10–13) and Echinoderms (Figs. 5, 7–9)

1–4.* **Arcoscalpellum quadratum** (J. de C. Sowerby). Barnacle. 1, carina; 2, tergum; 3, scutum (all ×2); 4, complete capitulum (×1½.) London Clay, Bognor Regis, Sussex. RANGE: London Clay.

5. **Archastropecten crispatus** (Forbes). Starfish. (×1.) London Clay, Sheppey, Kent. RANGE: London Clay.

6. **Xanthopsis leachi** (Desmarest). Crab. (×1.) London Clay, Chalk Farm, North London. RANGE: London Clay.

7.* **Ophiura wetherelli** Forbes. Brittle-Star (×1½.) London Clay, Bognor Regis, Sussex. RANGE: London Clay–Barton Beds.

8, 9.* **Isselicrinus subbasaltiformis** (Miller). Sea Lily. Stem ossicles and stem. (×2.) London Clay, Haverstock Hill, North London. RANGE: London Clay.

10.* **Xanthilites bowerbanki** Bell. Crab. (×1.) London Clay, Sheppey, Kent. RANGE: London Clay.

11.* **Dromilites lamarcki** (Desmarest). Crab. (×1.) London Clay, Sheppey, Kent. RANGE: London Clay.

12.* **Hoploparia gammaroides** McCoy. Lobster. (×1.) London Clay, Sheppey, Kent. RANGE: London Clay.

13. **Glyphithyreus [Plagiolophus] wetherelli** (Bell). Crab. (×1.) London Clay, Sheppey, Kent. RANGE: London Clay.

Plate 4

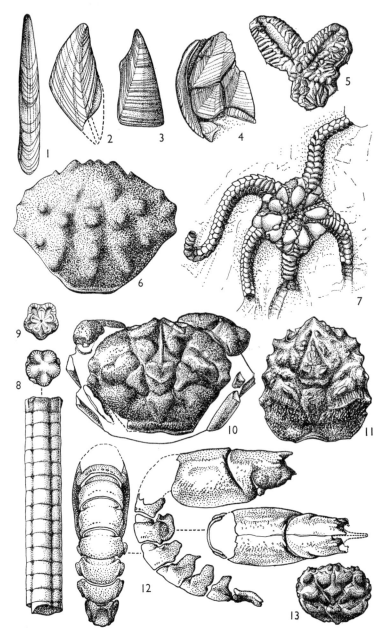

Plate 5

Eocene and Oligocene Bivalves

1, 2.* **Nucula similis** J. Sowerby. (× 1½.) Barton Beds: 1, Barton, Hants; 2, Alum Bay, Isle of Wight. RANGE: Barton Beds.

3, 4. **Nucula fragilis** Deshayes. (× 1½.) Blackheath Beds, Abbey Wood, Kent. RANGE: Blackheath Beds.

5, 6.* **Nuculana amygdaloides** (J. de C. Sowerby). (× 1½.) London Clay: 5, Potters Bar, Middlesex; 6, Chalk Farm, North London. RANGE: London Clay. [Syn., *Leda amygdaloides*.]

7, 8. **Trinacria curvirostris** Cossmann. (× 2.) Headon Beds, Headon Hill, Isle of Wight. RANGE: Barton Headon and Bembridge Beds. [Syn., *Trigonocoelia deltoidea* of authors.]

9.* **Glycymeris brevirostris** (J. de C. Sowerby). (× 1.) London Clay, Bognor Regis, Sussex. RANGE: London Clay. [Syn., *Pectunculus brevirostris*.]

10.* **Glycymeris plumstediensis** (J. Sowerby). (× 1.) Blackheath Beds, Abbey Wood, Kent. RANGE: Woolwich Beds–London Clay. [Syn., *Pectunculus plumstediensis, P. plumsteadiensis*.]

Plate 5

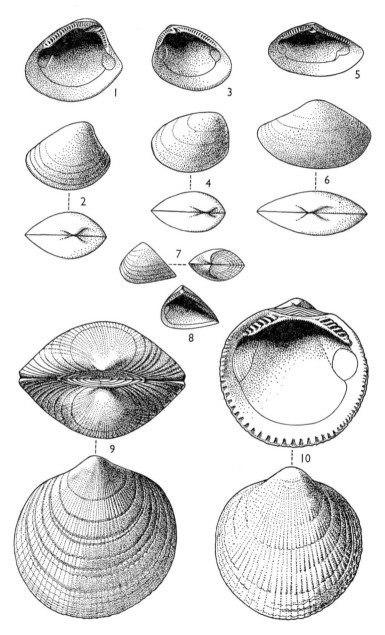

Plate 6

Eocene and Oligocene Bivalves

1, 2.* **Glycymeris wrigleyi** Curry. ($\times 1\frac{1}{2}$). London Clay, Highgate, North London. RANGE: London Clay. [Syn., *Pectunculus decussatus* J. Sowerby, *Glycymeris decussata*.]

3, 4.* **Musculus elegans** (J. Sowerby). 3, internal mould ($\times 1$); 4, shell ($\times 1\frac{1}{2}$). London Clay, Highgate, North London. RANGE: London Clay–Middle Headon Beds. [Syn., *Modiola elegans*.]

5, 6. **Limopsis scalaris** (J. de C. Sowerby). ($\times 1\frac{1}{2}$.) Barton Beds, Barton, Hants. RANGE: Barton Beds.

7. **Pteria media** (J. Sowerby). ($\times 1$.) London Clay, Bracknell, Berks. RANGE: Blackheath–Middle Headon Beds. [Syn., *Avicula media*.]

8, 9.* **Glycymeris deleta** (Solander). ($\times 1$.) Barton Beds, Barton, Hants. RANGE: Bracklesham–Barton Beds. [Syn., *Pectunculus deletus*.]

10.* **Arca biangula** Lamarck. ($\times \frac{3}{4}$.) Bracklesham Beds, Bracklesham Bay, Sussex. RANGE: Bracklesham Beds–Middle Headon Beds [Brockenhurst Bed].

Plate 6

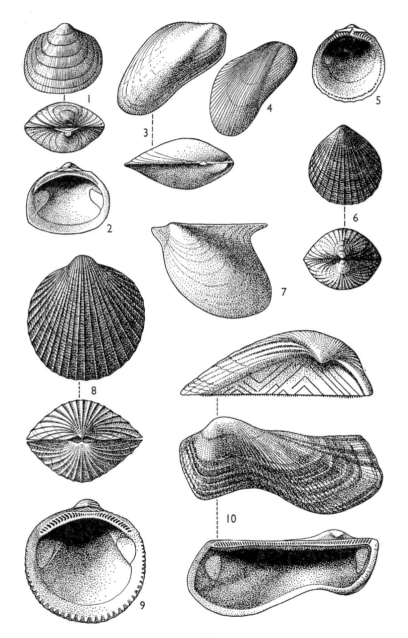

Plate 7

Eocene Bivalves

1.* **Pinna affinis** J. Sowerby. (×½.) London Clay, Fareham, Hants. RANGE: London Clay.

2.* **Chlamys recondita** (Solander). (×1½.) Barton Beds, Barton, Hants. RANGE: Upper Bracklesham–Barton Beds. [Syn., *Pecten reconditus.*]

3, 4. **Pecten duplicatus** J. de C. Sowerby. (×1.) 3, right valve; 4, left valve. London Clay, Haverstock Hill, North London. RANGE: London Clay. [Syn., *Chlamys woodi* Teppner.]

5.* **Amusium (Lentipecten) corneum** (J. Sowerby). (×¾.) Bracklesham Beds, Bracklesham Bay, Sussex. RANGE: London Clay–Barton Beds. [Syn., *Pecten corneus.*]

6, 7.* **Cucullaea decussata** Parkinson. (×1.) Thanet Sands, Herne Bay, Kent. RANGE: Thanet Sands–London Clay.

Plate 7

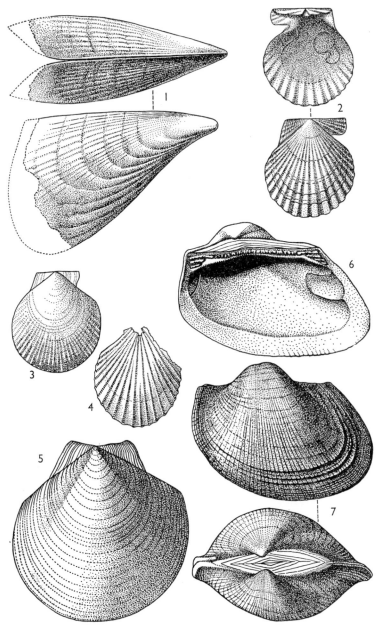

Plate 8

Eocene and Oligocene Bivalves

1, 2. **Ostrea velata** S. V. Wood. ($\times 1$.) Headon Beds, Colwell Bay, Isle of Wight. RANGE: Headon Beds.

3.* **Ostrea tenera** J. Sowerby. ($\times \frac{1}{2}$.) Blackheath Beds, Upnor, Kent. RANGE: Woolwich–Bracklesham Beds.

4, 5.* **Ostrea bellovacina** Lamarck. ($\times \frac{1}{2}$.) 4, Blackheath Beds, Sundridge, Kent; 5, Woolwich Beds, Croydon, Surrey. RANGE: Thanet Sands–Blackheath Beds.

Plate 8

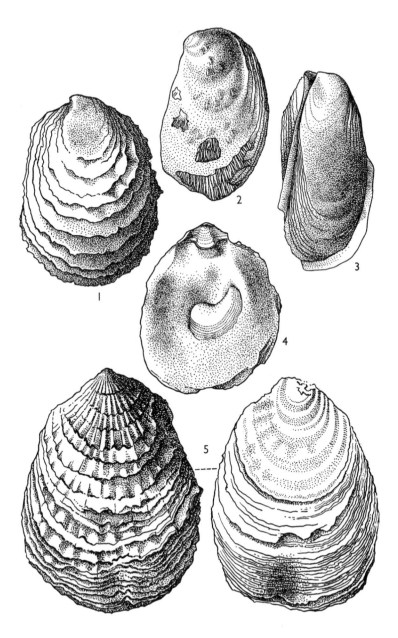

Plate 9

Eocene and Oligocene Bivalves

1.* **Ostrea plicata** Solander. (×1.) Barton Beds, Barton, Hants. RANGE: Bracklesham Beds–Headon Beds. [Syn., *Ostrea flabellula* Lamarck.]

2, 3.* **Astarte tenera** Morris. (×1.) Thanet Sands, Herne Bay, Kent. RANGE: Thanet Sands.

4. **Astarte filigera** S. V. Wood. (×1.) London Clay, Finchley, North London. RANGE: London Clay.

5. **Crassatella (Salaputium) aequalis** S. V. Wood. (×1.) Barton Beds, Barton, Hants. RANGE: Bracklesham–Barton Beds.

6.* **Glans oblonga** (J. Sowerby). (×1.) Barton Beds, Barton, Hants. RANGE: Bracklesham–Barton Beds. [Syn., *Venericardia oblonga*, *Cardita oblonga*.]

7, 8.* **Cardita sulcata** (Solander). (×1.) Barton Beds, Barton, Hants. RANGE: Barton Beds.

9, 10. **Crassatella compressa** Lamarck. (×1.) Upper Bracklesham Beds. Brook, Hants. RANGE: Bracklesham Beds.

11, 12.* **Crassatella sulcata** (Solander). (×1.) Barton Beds, Barton, Hants. RANGE: Barton Beds.

13, 14.* **Cardita deltoidea** (J. Sowerby). (×1.) Middle Headon Beds, Brockenhurst, Hants. RANGE: Headon Beds. [Syn., *Venericardia deltoidea*.]

15. **Cardita (Venericor) planicosta suessoniensis** (d'Archiac). (×1.) Lower Bracklesham Beds, Whitecliff Bay, Isle of Wight. RANGE: Bracklesham Beds.

16. **Crassatella sowerbyi** S. V. Wood. (×1.) Upper Bracklesham Beds, Stubbington, Hants. RANGE: Bracklesham Beds.

Plate 9

Plate 10

Eocene and Oligocene Bivalves

1, 2, 3.* **Polymesoda convexa** (Brongniart). (×1.) Hamstead Beds, Hamstead, Isle of Wight. RANGE: Bembridge–Hamstead Beds. [Syn., *Cyrena convexa*, *Cyrena semistriata* Deshayes.]

4, 5. **Corbicula (Tellinocyclas) tellinoides** (Férussac). (×1.) Blackheath Beds, Abbey Wood, Kent. RANGE: Woolwich–Blackheath Beds. [Syn., *Cyrena tellinella* Deshayes.]

6–8.* **Corbicula cuneiformis** (J. Sowerby). (×1.) Woolwich Beds, Upnor, Kent. RANGE: Woolwich–Blackheath Beds. [Syn., *Cyrena cuneiformis.*]

9, 10.* **Cardita (Venericor) planicosta** (Lamarck). (×½.) Bracklesham Beds, Bracklesham, Sussex. RANGE: Bracklesham–Barton Beds. [Syn., *Venericardia planicosta.*]

11, 12.* **Corbicula cordata** (Morris). (×1.) Woolwich Beds, Charlton, South-east London, RANGE: Woolwich Beds. [Syn., *Cyrena cordata.*]

Plate 10

Plate 11

Eocene and Oligocene Bivalves

1. **Corbicula obovata** (J. Sowerby). (×1.) Upper Headon Beds, Colwell Bay, Isle of Wight. RANGE: Headon Beds. [Syn., *Cyrena obovata.*]

2, 3.* **Chama squamosa** Solander. (×1.) Barton Beds, Barton, Hants. RANGE: Barton Beds.

4, 5.* **Arctica morrisi** (J. de C. Sowerby). (×1.) Oldhaven Beds, High Halstow, Kent. RANGE: Thanet Sands–London Clay. [Syn., *Cyprina morrisi.*]

6.* **Nemocardium nitens** (J. Sowerby). (×1½.) London Clay, Down Mill, Bracknell, Berks. RANGE: London Clay. [Syn., *Cardium nitens, Protocardia nitens.*]

7.* **Arctica planata** (J. de C. Sowerby). (×1.) London Clay, Portsmouth, Hants. RANGE: Woolwich Beds–Middle Headon Beds. [Syn., *Cyprina planata, C. scutellaria* of authors.]

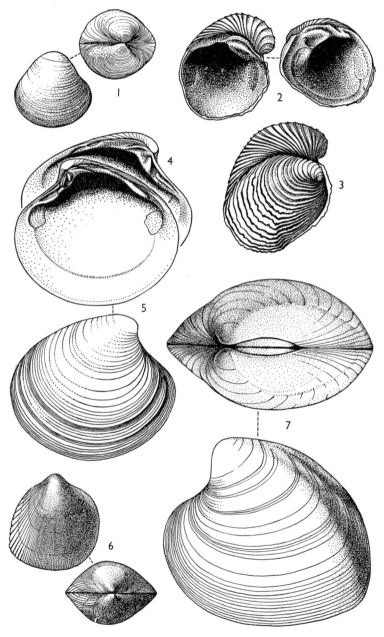

Plate 11

Plate 12

Eocene and Oligocene Bivalves

1–3.* **Costacallista laevigata** (Lamarck). 1, (×¾); 2, (×1); 3, (×1¼). Upper Bracklesham Beds, Stubbington, Hants. RANGE: Bracklesham–Headon Beds. [Syn., *Cytherea laevigata*.]

4, 5. **Nemocardium turgidum** (Solander). (×1½.) Barton Beds, Barton, Hants. RANGE: Barton Beds. [Syn., *Cardium turgidum*.]

6–8.* **Sinodia (Cordiopsis) suborbicularis** (Goldfuss). (×¾.) Middle Headon Beds, Colwell Bay, Isle of Wight. RANGE: Barton Beds–Bembridge Beds. [Syn., *Venus incrassata* J. Sowerby, *Cytherea incrassata, Cordiopsis incrassata*.]

9. **Thyasira angulata** (J. Sowerby). (×1.) London Clay, Lambeth Hill, City of London. RANGE: London Clay. [Syn., *Axinus angulatus*.]

10, 11.* **Nemocardium plumstedianum** (J. Sowerby). (×1) Blackheath Beds, Abbey Wood, Kent. RANGE: Thanet Sands–London Clay Basement Bed. [*Syn., Cardium plumstedianum*.]

12. **Thyasira goodhalli** (J. de C. Sowerby). (×1.) London Clay, Whetstone, North London. RANGE: London Clay. [Syn., *Cryptodon goodhalli, Axinus goodhalli*.]

13.* **Cardium (Orthocardium) porulosum** Solander. (×1.) Barton Beds, Barton, Hants. RANGE: Bracklesham–Headon Beds.

Plate 12

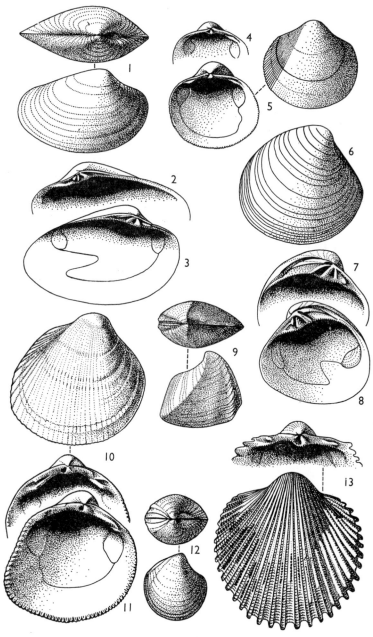

55

Plate 13

Eocene Bivalves

1-3.* **Pitar (Calpitaria) sulcatarius** (Deshayes). (×1.) London Clay: 1, 3, Portsmouth, Hants; 2, Highgate, North London. RANGE: London Clay–Barton Beds. [Syn., *Cytherea tenuistriata* (J. de C. Sowerby), *Cytherea suessoniensis* Watelet.]

4-6. **Callista (Microcallista) proxima** (Deshayes). (×1.) London Clay, Portsmouth Dock, Hants. RANGE: London Clay–Lower Bracklesham Beds. [Syn., *Cytherea proxima, Meretrix proxima.*]

7, 8. **Callista (Microcallista) heberti belgica** Vincent. (Exterior, ×1; hinge-teeth, ×1½). Barton Beds, Barton, Hants. RANGE: Barton Beds. [Syn., *Venus elegans* J. de C. Sowerby.]

9-11.* **Dosinopsis bellovacina** (Deshayes). (×1.) Thanet Sands, Herne Bay, Kent. RANGE: Thanet Sands–London Clay Basement Bed. [Syn., *Cytherea orbicularis* Morris.]

12. 13. **Pitar (Calpitaria) obliquus** (Deshayes). (×1.) Blackheath Beds, Swanscombe, Kent. RANGE: Woolwich Beds–London Clay Basement Bed. [Syn., *Cytherea obliqua, Meretrix obliqua.*]

Plate 13

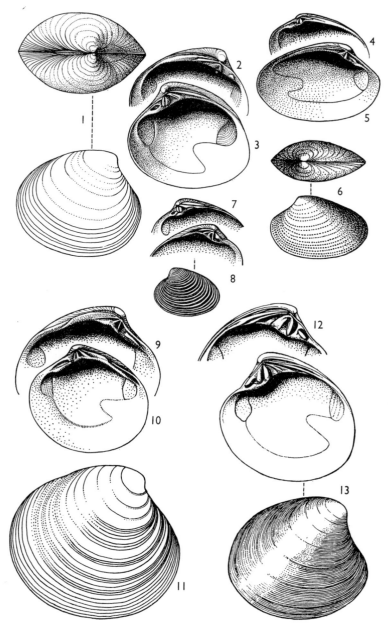

Plate 14
Eocene and Oligocene Bivalves

1. **Lentidium tawneyi** Curry (×3.) Upper Barton Beds, Long Mead End, Hants. RANGE: Barton–Headon Beds. [Syn., *Corbula nitida* of authors.]

2. **Cultellus affinis** (J. Sowerby). (×1.) London Clay, Highgate, North London. RANGE: London Clay–Barton Beds.

3–5.* **Erodona plana** (J.Sowerby). (×1.) Middle Headon Beds, Hordle, Hants. RANGE: Barton–Headon Beds. [Syn., *Potamomya plana*.]

6. **Abra splendens** (J. de C. Sowerby). (×3.) London Clay, Highgate, North London. RANGE: London Clay. [Syn., *Syndosmya splendens*.]

7–9. **Corbula plicata** Wrigley. (×1½.) Upper Bracklesham Beds, Brook, Hants. RANGE: Upper Bracklesham Beds.

10. **Corbula pisum** J. Sowerby. (×3.) Upper Bracklesham Beds, Brook, Hants. RANGE: Bracklesham–Headon Beds.

11–13.* **Corbula regulbiensis** Morris (×2.) Thanet Sands: 11, Herne Bay, Kent; 12, 13, Richborough, Kent. RANGE: Thanet Sands.

14. **Corbula cuspidata** J. Sowerby. (×2.) Middle Headon Beds, Brockenhurst, Hants. RANGE: Upper Barton–Headon Beds.

15.* **Corbula ficus** (Solander). (×1.) Barton Beds, Barton, Hants. RANGE: Barton Beds.

16–18.* **Corbula (Bicorbula) gallica** Lamarck. (×1.) Bracklesham Beds, Bracklesham Bay, Sussex. RANGE: Bracklesham Beds.

Plate 14

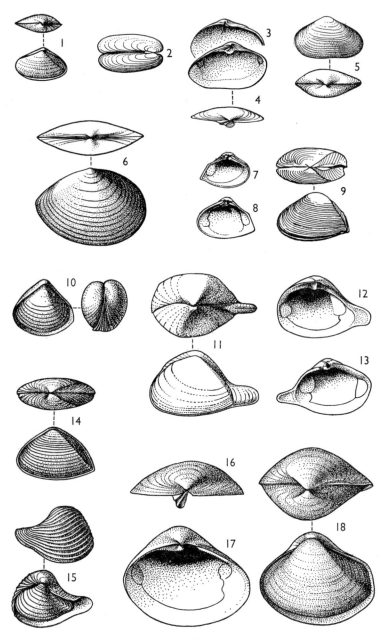

Plate 15

Eocene and Oligocene Bivalves

1.* **Thracia oblata** (J. de C. Sowerby). (×¾.) Thanet Sands, Herne Bay, Kent. RANGE: Thanet Sands–London Clay.

2–4.* **Psammotaea compressa** (J. de C. Sowerby). (×1.) Barton Beds, Barton, Hants. RANGE: Bracklesham–Headon Beds. [Syn., *Sanguinolaria compressa, Psammobia compressa.*]

5. **Garum edvardsi** (Morris). (×¾.) Thanet Sands, Herne Bay, Kent. RANGE: Thanet Sands. [Syn., *Sanguinolaria edwardsi* of authors.]

6–8.* **Macrosolen hollowaysi** (J. Sowerby). (×¾.) Bracklesham Beds, Bracklesham, Sussex. RANGE: Bracklesham Beds. [Syn., *Sanguinolaria hollowaysi.*]

9, 10. **Garum rude** (Lamarck). (×¾.) Headon Beds, Colwell Bay, Isle of Wight. RANGE: Barton–Headon Beds.

11, 12.* **Cyrtodaria rutupiensis** (Morris). (×¾.) Thanet Sands, Herne Bay, Kent. RANGE: Thanet Sands.

Plate 15

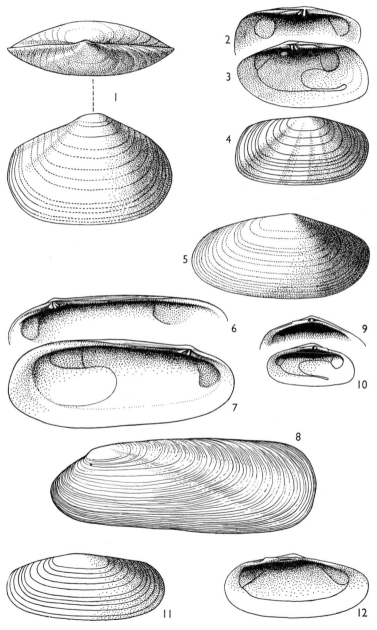

Plate 16

Eocene and Oligocene Bivalves

1–3.* **Teredina personata** (Lamarck). Ship-worm. London Clay; 1, Highgate, North London (×4); 2 ?Highgate, North London (×1); 3, Tolworth, Surrey (×¾). RANGE: Woolwich Beds–London Clay.

4. **Eutylus cuneatus** (Morris). (×¾.) Thanet Sands, Herne Bay, Kent. RANGE: Thanet Sands. [Syn., *Pholadomya cuneata.*]

5.* **Panopea intermedia** (J. Sowerby). (×1.) London Clay, Portsmouth, Hants. RANGE: Blackheath–Headon Beds.

6.* **Pholadomya margaritacea** (J. Sowerby). (×1.) London Clay, Alum Bay, Isle of Wight. RANGE: London Clay.

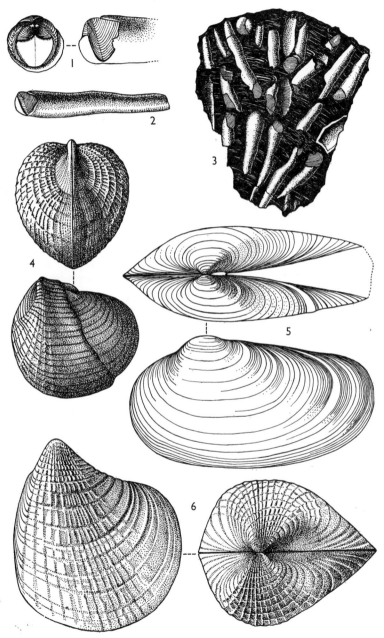

Plate 16

Plate 17

Eocene and Oligocene Gastropods

1.* **Calliostoma nodulosum** (Solander). (×1.) Barton Beds, Barton, Hants. RANGE: Barton Beds. [Syn., *Trochus nodulosus*.]

2, 3. **Theodoxus apertus** (J. de C. Sowerby). (×2.) 2, operculum, (*a*, outer and *b*, inner faces) Headon Beds, Colwell Bay, Isle of Wight. RANGE: Headon Beds. [Syn., *Neritina aperta*.]

4.* **Theodoxus concavus** (J. de C. Sowerby). (×2.) Headon Beds, Headon Hill, Isle of Wight. RANGE: Headon–Hamstead Beds. [Syn., *Neritina concava*.]

5. **Rostreulima macrostoma** (Charlesworth). (×7½.) Barton Beds, Barton, Hants. RANGE: Barton Beds. [Syn., *Eulima macrostoma*.]

6.* **Epitonium (Acrilla) reticulatum** (Solander). (×1½.) Barton Beds, Barton, Hants. RANGE: Bracklesham–Barton Beds. [Syn., *Scala reticulata*.]

7. **Solariaxis pulcher** (J. de C. Sowerby). (*a–c*, ×1; *d*, sculpture of base, ×3; *e*, sculpture of spire, ×3.) London Clay, Highgate, North London, RANGE: London Clay–Bracklesham Beds. [Syn., *Solarium pulchrum*.]

8, 9. **Melanella (Polygireulima) polygyra** (Charlesworth). (8, shell, ×7½, 9, apex, much enlarged.) Lower Barton Beds, Barton, Hants. RANGE: Barton Beds. [Syn., *Eulima polygyra, E. politissima* Newton.]

10.* **Calyptraea aperta** (Solander). (×1.) Barton Beds, Barton, Hants. RANGE: Woolwich–Headon Beds.

11. **Architectonica bonneti** (Cossmann). (×1½.) Barton Beds, Barton, Hants. RANGE: Barton Beds. [Syn., *Solarium bonneti, S. plicatum* of English authors.]

12. **Nystia duchasteli** (Nyst). (×2.) Hamstead Beds, Hamstead, Isle of Wight. RANGE: Hamstead Beds. [Syn., *Tomichia duchasteli*.]

13. **Viviparus angulosus** (J. Sowerby). (×1.) Bembridge Beds, Sconce, Isle of Wight. RANGE: Headon–Bembridge Beds. [Syn., *Paludina angulosa*.]

14.* **Viviparus lentus** (Solander). (×1.) Headon Beds, Headon, Isle of Wight. RANGE: Headon–Hamstead Beds. [Syn., *Paludina lenta*.]

15.* **Xenophora extensa** (J. Sowerby). (×1.) London Clay, Highgate, North London. RANGE: London Clay.

Plate 17

Plate 18

Eocene and Oligocene Gastropods

1. **Sigatica abducta** (Deshayes). (× 1.) Blackheath Beds, Bickley, Kent. RANGE: Thanet Sands–London Clay Basement Bed. [Syn., *Natica abducta.*]

2.* **Euspira glaucinoides** (J. Sowerby). (× 1.) London Clay, Clarendon, Wilts. RANGE: Blackheath Beds–London Clay. [Syn., *Natica glaucinoides.*]

3. **Euspira bartonensis** Wrigley. (× 1.) Middle Barton Beds, Barton, Hants. RANGE: Barton Beds.

4. **Ampullonatica ambulacrum** (J. Sowerby). (× 1.) Upper Barton Beds, Barton, Hants. RANGE: Upper Bracklesham–Barton Beds. [Syn., *Natica ambulacrum.*]

5, 6. **Euspira bassae** Wrigley. (× 1.) 5, Thanet Sands, Bishopstone, near Herne Bay, Kent; 6, corroded shell. Blackheath Beds, Bickley, Kent. RANGE: Thanet Sands–Blackheath Beds.

7. **Globularia grossa** (Deshayes). (× 1.) Middle Barton Beds, Barton, Hants. RANGE: Upper Bracklesham–Middle Headon Beds. [Syn., *Ampullina grossa.*]

8.* **Globularia patula** (Lamarck). (× 1.) Middle Barton Beds, Barton, Hants. RANGE: Bracklesham–Barton Beds. [Syn., *Ampullina patula.*]

9. **Globularia sigaretina** (Lamarck). (× 1.) Middle Barton Beds, Barton, Hants. RANGE: Bracklesham–Barton Beds. [Syn., *Ampullina sigaretina.*]

10.* **Crommium willemeti** (Deshayes). (× 1.) Upper Bracklesham Beds, Bramshaw, Hants. RANGE: Bracklesham Beds. [Syn., *Ampullina willemeti.*]

11. **Xenophora agglutinans** (Lamarck), (× 1.) Upper Bracklesham Beds, Bramshaw, Hants. RANGE: Bracklesham–Barton Beds.

Plate 18

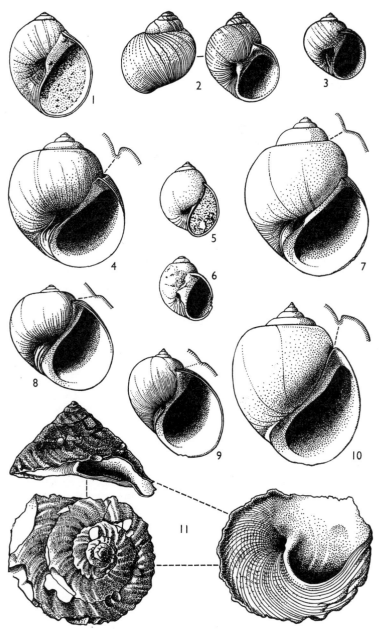

Plate 19
Eocene and Oligocene Gastropods

1. **Orthochetus elongatus** Wrigley. ($\times 1\frac{1}{2}$.) London Clay, Whetstone, North London. RANGE: London Clay.

2. **Melanoides (Tarebia) acuta** (J. Sowerby). ($\times 2$.) Headon Beds, Headon Hill, Isle of Wight. RANGE: Headon–Hamstead Beds, [Syn., *Melania acuta, M. muricata* Forbes.]

3, 4.* **Potamides (Ptychopotamides) vagus** (Solander). ($\times 1$.) Lower Headon Beds, Hordle, Hants. RANGE: Headon Beds.

5.* **Tympanotonos funatus** (J. Sowerby). ($\times 1$.) Woolwich Beds, New-haven, Sussex. RANGE: Woolwich–Blackheath Beds. [Syn., *Potamides funatus.*]

6. **Pirenella monilifera** (Defrance). ($\times 1\frac{1}{2}$.) Hamstead Beds, Ham-stead, Isle of Wight. RANGE: Hamstead Beds. [Syn., *Cerithium plicatum, Terebralia plicata* of authors.]

7. **Mesalia sulcata** (Lamarck). ($\times 1$.) Bracklesham Beds, Brackle-sham, Sussex. RANGE: Bracklesham Beds.

8. **Melanopsis antidiluviana** (Poiret). ($\times 1$.) Blackheath Beds, Abbey Wood, Kent. RANGE: Woolwich–Blackheath Beds. [Syn., *Melanopsis buccinoidea* Férussac.]

9. **Potamaclis turritissima** (Forbes). ($\times 3$.) Hamstead Beds, Ham-stead, Isle of Wight. RANGE: Headon–Hamstead Beds.

10.* **Batillaria concava** (J. Sowerby). ($\times 1$.) Headon Beds, Headon Hill, Isle of Wight. RANGE: Barton–Headon Beds. [Syn., *Potamides concavus.*]

11.* **Turritella (Haustator) imbricataria** Lamarck. ($\times 1$.) Upper Bracklesham Beds, Bramshaw, Hants. RANGE: Bracklesham: Barton Beds.

12.* **Turritella (Ispharina) sulcifera** Deshayes. ($\times \frac{1}{2}$.) Bracklesham Beds, Bracklesham, Sussex, RANGE: London Clay–Bracklesham Beds.

13, 14.* **Brotia melanioides** (J. Sowerby). ($\times 1$.) 13, Woolwich Beds, Charlton, South-east London; 14, Pourcy, near Paris—to show labral profile. RANGE: Woolwich–Blackheath Beds. [Syn., *Melania inquinata* Defrance, *Melanatria inquinata* (Defrance).]

15, 16. **Batillaria ventricosa** (J. Sowerby). ($\times 2$.) Headon Beds, Hordle, Hants. RANGE: Headon Beds. [Syn., *Potamides ventricosus.*]

17.* **Turritella edita** (Solander). ($\times 1$.) Barton Beds, Barton, Hants. RANGE: Bracklesham–Barton Beds.

18. **Sigatica hantoniensis** (Pilkington). ($\times 1$.) London Clay, Ports-mouth, Hants. RANGE: London–Clay Middle Headon Beds. [Syn., *Natica hantoniensis.*]

Plate 19

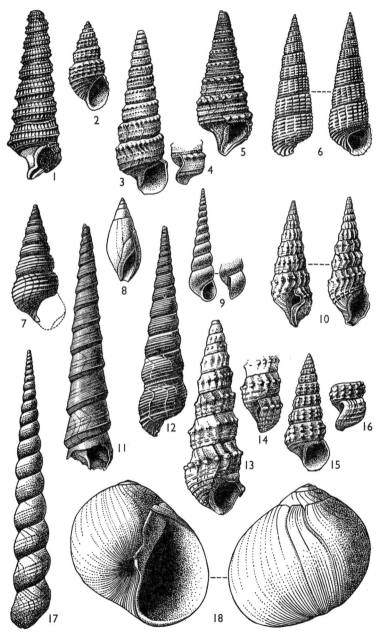

Plate 20
Eocene and Oligocene Gastropods

1. **Aporrhais triangulata** Gardner. (×1.) Blackheath Beds, West of Oldhaven Gap, Herne Bay, Kent. RANGE: Blackheath Beds–London Clay Basement Bed.

2.* **Rimella rimosa** (Solander). (×1.) Barton Beds, Barton, Hants. RANGE: Barton–Middle Headon Beds.

3, 4.* **Tibia lucida** (J. Sowerby). (×1½.) 3, juvenile shell. London Clay, Highgate, North London. RANGE: London Clay. [Syn., *Rostellaria lucida*.]

5, 6.* **Aporrhais sowerbii** (Fleming). (×1½.) London Clay: 5, Highgate, North London; 6, Tolworth, Surrey. RANGE: London Clay.

7. **Dientomochilus bartonense** (J. Sowerby). (×1½.) Lower Barton Beds, Highcliffe, Hants. RANGE: Lower Barton Beds. [Syn., *Strombus bartonensis*.]

8.* **Terebellum (Seraphs) sopitum** (Solander). (×¾.) Barton Beds, Barton, Hants. RANGE: Upper Bracklesham–Headon Beds.

9. **Ectinochilus planum** (Beyrich). (×1½.) Upper Bracklesham Beds, Huntingbridge, Hants. RANGE: Upper Bracklesham–Barton Beds. [Syn., *Rimella canalis* of authors.]

10.* **Hippochrenes amplus** (Solander). (×⅓.) Middle Barton Beds, Barton, Hants. RANGE: London Clay–Barton Beds. [Syn., *Rostellaria ampla, Hippochrenes incertus* Wrigley.]

Plate 20

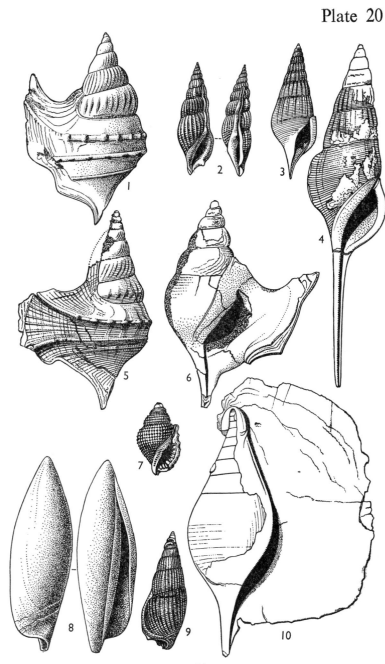

Plate 21

Eocene Gastropods

1. **Ficus nexilis** (Solander). (×1½.) Middle Barton Beds, Barton Hants. RANGE: Upper Bracklesham–Barton Beds. [Syn., *Pyrula nexilis*.]

2, 3. **Ficus (Priscoficus) multiformis** Wrigley. (×1½.) London Clay, near Finchley, North London. RANGE: London Clay.

4.* **Galeodea gallica** Wrigley. (×1½.) London Clay, Highgate, North London. RANGE: London Clay.

5. **Campanile cornucopiae** (J. Sowerby). (×½.) Upper Bracklesham Beds, Stubbington, Hants. RANGE: Bracklesham Beds.

6.* **Ficus (Priscoficus) smithi** (J. de C. Sowerby). (×¾.) London Clay, Portsmouth Dock, Hants. RANGE: London Clay. [Syn., *Pyrula smithi*.]

Plate 21

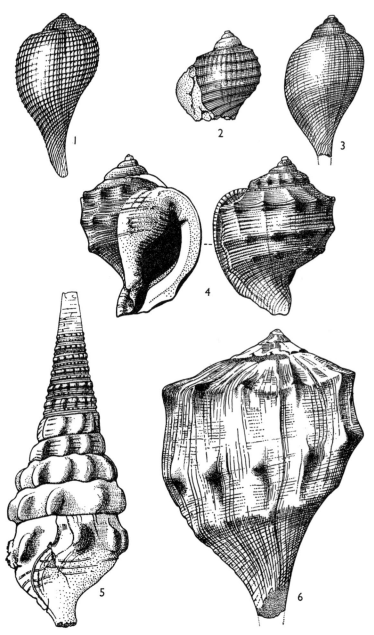

Plate 22

Eocene and Oligocene Gastropods

1.* **Pseudoliva fissurata** (Deshayes). (×1.) Blackheath Beds, Abbey Wood, Kent. RANGE: Woolwich Beds–London Clay.

2, 3. **Siphonalia subnodosa** (Morris). (×1¼.) Blackheath Beds: 2, Bishopstone, near Herne Bay, Kent; 3, Swanscombe Hill, Kent. RANGE: Thanet Sands–London Clay Basement Bed. [Syn., *Trophon subnodosum.*]

4.* **Sassia arguta** (Solander). (×1½.) Middle Barton Beds, Barton, Hants. RANGE: Bracklesham–Barton Beds. [Syn., *Triton argutus.*]

5.* **Sconsia ambigua** (Solander). (×1½.) Lower Barton Beds, Barton, Hants. RANGE: Barton–Middle Headon Beds. [Syn., *Cassis ambigua.*]

6.* **Pollia labiata** (J. de C. Sowerby). (×1.) Middle Headon Beds, Brockenhurst, Hants. RANGE: Bracklesham–Headon Beds. [Syn., *Pisania labiata.*]

7.* **Galeodea coronata** (Deshayes). (×1½.) Upper Bracklesham Beds, Brook, Hants. RANGE: Bracklesham Beds. [Syn., *Cassidaria coronata.*]

Plate 22

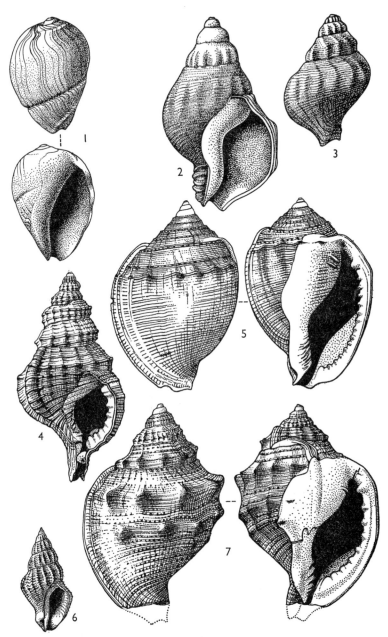

Plate 23

Eocene and Oligocene Gastropods

1. **Pollia londini** (Wrigley). ($\times 1\frac{1}{4}$.) London Clay, Finchley, North London. RANGE: London Clay. [Syn., *Tritonidea londini.*]

2.* **Pterynotus tricarinatus** (Lamarck). ($\times 1\frac{1}{2}$.) Middle Barton Beds, Barton, Hants. RANGE: Upper Bracklesham–Barton Beds. [Syn., *Murex tricarinatus.*]

3.* **Typhis pungens** (Solander). ($\times 1\frac{1}{2}$.) Barton Beds, Barton, Hants. RANGE: Upper Bracklesham–Middle Headon Beds.

4. **Pterynotus hantoniensis** (Edwards). ($\times 1\frac{1}{2}$.) Middle Headon Beds, Brockenhurst, Hants. RANGE: Middle Headon Beds. [Syn., *Murex hantoniensis.*]

5, 6.* **Clavilithes macrospira** Cossmann. 5, initial whorls enlarged; 6, ($\times 1$.) Barton Beds, Barton, Hants. RANGE: Bracklesham–Barton Beds.

7. **Urosalpinx sexdentatus** (J. de C. Sowerby). ($\times 1\frac{1}{2}$.) Middle Headon Beds, Colwell Bay, Isle of Wight. RANGE: Barton–Headon Beds. [Syn., *Murex sexdentatus.*]

8. **Fusinus asper** (J. Sowerby). *a,* ($\times 1\frac{1}{2}$); *b,* initial whorls of another specimen, enlarged. Barton Beds, Barton, Hants. RANGE: Barton Beds. [Syn., *Fusus asper.*]

9. **Bartonia canaliculata** (J. de C. Sowerby). ($\times 1\frac{1}{2}$.) Lower Barton Beds, Barton, Hants. RANGE: Barton Beds. [Syn., *Cominella canaliculata.*]

10.* **Clavilithes longaevus** (Solander). ($\times \frac{1}{2}$.) Barton Beds, Barton, Hants. RANGE: Bracklesham–Barton Beds. [Syn., *Fusus longaevus.*]

11.* **Fusinus porrectus** (Solander). *a,* ($\times 2$); *b,* initial whorls enlarged. Upper Barton Beds, Barton, Hants. RANGE: Bracklesham Beds–Upper Barton Beds. [Syn., *Fusus porrectus.*]

12. **Fusinus wetherelli** Wrigley. ($\times 1$.) London Clay, Finchley, North London. RANGE: London Clay.

Plate 23

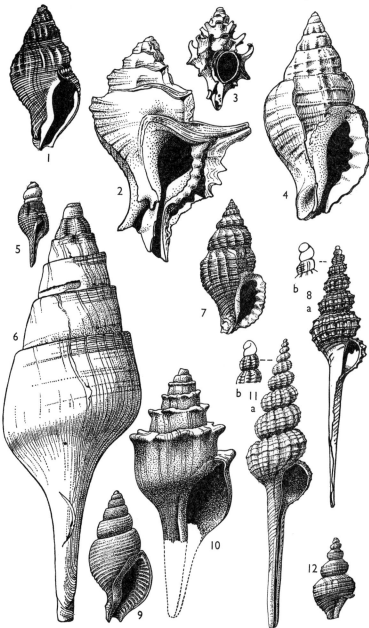

Plate 24

Eocene and Oligocene Gastropods

1. **Streptolathyrus zonulatus** Wrigley. (× 1¾.) London Clay, Highgate, North London. RANGE: London Clay.

2. **Euthriofusus transversarius** Wrigley. (× 1½.) London Clay, Highgate, North London. RANGE: London Clay.

3. **Streptolathyrus cymatodis** (Edwards). (× 1.) London Clay, Clarendon, Wilts. RANGE: London Clay.

4.* **Euthriofusus complanatus** (J. de C. Sowerby). (× 1.) London Clay, Highgate, North London. RANGE: London Clay. [Syn., *Fusus complanatus.*]

5.* **Sycostoma pyrus** (Solander). (× 1.) Barton Beds, Barton, Hants. RANGE: Bracklesham–Barton Beds. [Syn., *Leiostoma pyrus*, *Sycum pyrus.*]

6.* **Pseudoneptunea curta** (J. de C. Sowerby). (× 1½.) London Clay, Fareham, Hants. RANGE: London Clay. [Syn., *Pisania curta.*]

7.* **Strepsidura turgida** (Solander). (× 1.) Upper Bracklesham Beds, Brook, Hants. RANGE: Bracklesham–Barton Beds.

8.* **Volutocorbis scabricula** (Solander). (× 1.) Barton Beds, Barton, Hants. RANGE: Barton Beds. [Syn., *Voluta lima* J. de C. Sowerby.]

9. **Athleta (Neoathleta) rathieri** (Hébert). (× 1.) Hamstead Beds, Hamstead, Isle of Wight. RANGE: Hamstead Beds. [Syn., *Voluta rathieri.*]

10.* **Surculites errans** (Solander). (× 1½.) London Clay, near Chalk Farm, North London. RANGE: London Clay–Barton Beds, [Syn., *Fusus errans*, *Chrysodomus errans*, *Fusus bifaciatus* J. Sowerby, *Chrysodomus bifasciatus* of authors.]

11.* **Euthriofusus regularis** (J. Sowerby). (× 1.) Barton Beds, Barton, Hants. RANGE: Upper Bracklesham Beds–Barton Beds. [Syn., *Fusus regularis*, *Chrysodomus antiquus* (Solander).]

12. **Volutocorbis ambigua** (Solander). (× 1.) Middle Barton Beds, Barton Hants., RANGE: Barton Beds. [Syn., *Voluta ambigua.*]

13.* **Cornulina minax** (Solander). (× 1.) Barton Beds, Barton, Hants. RANGE: Bracklesham–Middle Headon Beds. [Syn., *Murex minax.*]

Plate 24

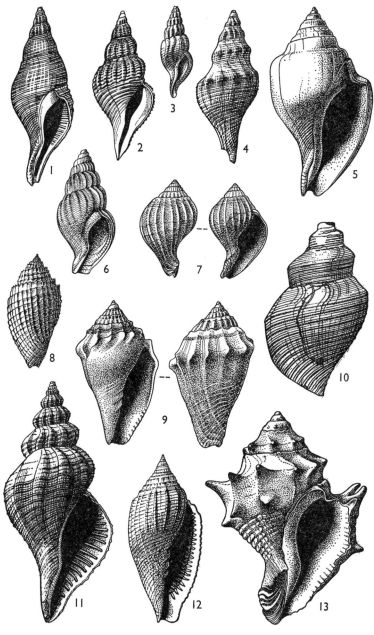

Plate 25
Eocene and Oligocene Gastropods

1. **Athleta (Volutospina) scalaris** (J. de C. Sowerby). (×1.) Barton Beds, Barton, Hants. RANGE: Barton Beds. [Syn., *Voluta scalaris.*]

2.* **Athleta (Volutospina) spinosus** (Linné). (×1.) Upper Bracklesham Beds, Brook, Hants. RANGE: Bracklesham–Headon Beds. [Syn., *Voluta spinosa.*]

3. **Lyria decora** (Beyrich). (×1.) Middle Headon Beds, Brockenhurst, Hants. RANGE: Bracklesham–Headon Beds. [Syn., *Voluta maga* Edwards.]

4. **Athleta selseiensis** (Edwards). (×1.) Upper Bracklesham Beds, Brook, Hants. RANGE: Bracklesham Beds. [Syn., *Voluta selseiensis.*]

5.* **Athleta (Volutospina) denudatus** (J. de C. Sowerby). (×1.) London Clay, Bognor Regis, Sussex. RANGE: London Clay, [Syn., *Voluta denudata.*]

6. **Conomitra parva** (J. de C. Sowerby). (×2.) Lower Barton Beds, Highcliffe, Hants. RANGE: Bracklesham–Barton Beds. [Syn., *Mitra parva.*]

7. **Athleta (Volutospina) nodosus** (J. de C. Sowerby). (×1.) London Clay, Highgate, North London. RANGE: London Clay–Barton Beds. [Syn., *Voluta nodosa.*]

8–10.* **Athleta (Volutospina) luctator** (Solander). 8, (×1); 9 initial, whorls (×10); 10, young shell (×1). Barton Beds, Barton, Hants. RANGE: Barton Beds. [Syn., *Voluta luctatrix.*]

Plate 25

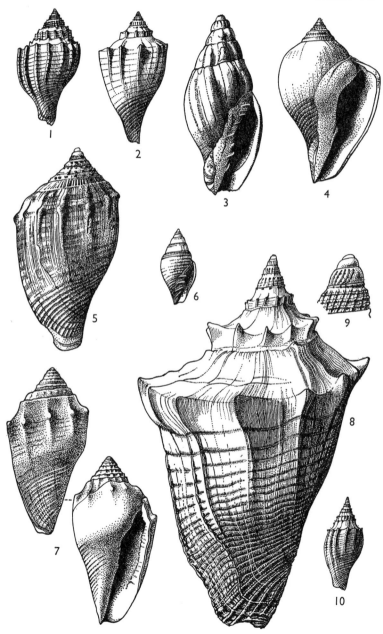

Plate 26
Eocene and Oligocene Gastropods

1.* **Ancilla canalifera** Lamarck. (× 1.) Barton Beds, Barton, Hants. RANGE: Bracklesham–Barton Beds.
2.* **Conorbis dormitor** (Solander). (× 1.) Barton Beds, Barton, Hants. RANGE: Barton Beds.
3.* **Olivella (Callianax) branderi** (J. Sowerby). (× 1.) Barton Beds, Barton, Hants. RANGE: Bracklesham–Barton Beds. [Syn., *Oliva branderi.*]
   4. **Bonellitia laeviuscula** (J. Sowerby). (× 2.) London Clay, Highgate, North London. RANGE: London Clay. [Syn., *Cancellaria laeviuscula.*]
   5. **Marginella (Stazzania) bifidoplicata** Charlesworth. (× 6.) Lower Barton Beds, Highcliffe, Hants. RANGE: Bracklesham–Barton Beds.
   6. **Sveltella microstoma** (Charlesworth). (× 2.) Barton Beds, Barton, Hants. RANGE: Upper Bracklesham–Barton Beds. [Syn., *Cancellaria microstoma.*]
7.* **Bonellitia evulsa** (Solander). (× 1.) Middle Barton Beds, Barton, Hants. RANGE: Barton Beds. [Syn., *Cancellaria evulsa.*]
8.* **Mitreola scabra** (J. de C. Sowerby). (× 1.) Barton Beds, Barton, Hant. RANGE: Barton Beds. [Syn., *Mitra scabra.*]
   9. **Coptostoma quadratum** (J. Sowerby). (× 2.) Lower Barton Beds, Highcliffe, Hants. RANGE: Barton Beds. [Syn., *Cancellaria quadrata.*]
10.* **Turricula rostrata** (Solander). (× 1.) Barton Beds, Barton, Hants. RANGE: Barton Beds. [Syn., *Pleurotoma rostrata.*]
   11. **Turricula teretrium** (Edwards). (× 1.) London Clay, Highgate, London. RANGE: London Clay. [Syn., *Pleurotoma teretrium.*]
   12. **Unitas nassaeformis** (Wrigley). (× 2½.) Barton Beds, Barton, Hants. RANGE: Upper Bracklesham–Barton Beds. [Syn., *Uxia nassaeformis.*]
   13. **Bonellitia pyrgota** (Edwards). (× 1.) Middle Headon Beds, Colwell Bay, Isle of Wight. RANGE: Middle Headon Beds. [Syn., *Cancellaria pyrgota.*]
14, 15. **Hastula plicatula** (Lamarck). (× 2.) 15, showing colour banding. Blackheath Beds, Abbey Wood, Kent. RANGE: Blackheath–Barton Beds. [Syn., *Terebra plicatula.*]
16, 17.* **Bathytoma turbida** (Solander). (× 1.) Barton Beds, Barton, Hants. RANGE: Barton Beds. [Syn., *Pleurotoma turbida.*]
   18. **Athleta (Volutospina) athleta** (Solander). (× ¾.) Barton Beds, Barton Hants. RANGE: Bracklesham–Barton Beds. [Syn., *Voluta athleta.*]
   19. **Eopleurotoma simillima** (Edwards). (× 1½.) London Clay, Clarendon, Wilts. RANGE: London Clay. [Syn., *Pleurotoma simillima.*]

Plate 26

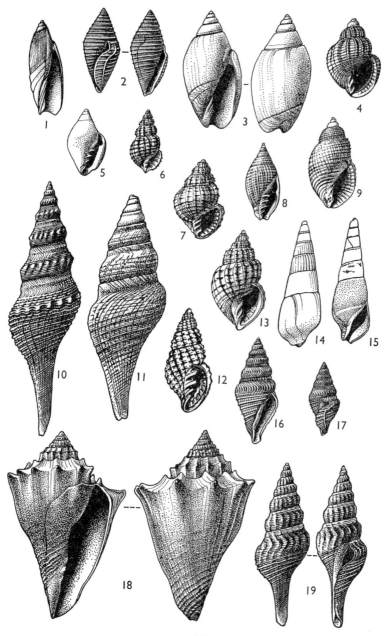

Plate 27

Eocene and Oligocene Gastropods

1. **Palaeoxestina occlusa** (Edwards). (×1.) Bembridge Limestone, Headon Hill, Isle of Wight. RANGE: Bembridge Beds. [Syn., *Helix occlusa.*]

2. **Megalocochlea pseudoglobosa** (d'Orbigny). (×½.) Bembridge Limestone, Tapnell, near Freshwater, Isle of Wight. RANGE: Bembridge Beds. [Syn., *Helix pseudoglobsa.*]

3.* **Klikia vectiensis** (Edwards). (×1½.) Bembridge Limestone, Headon Hill, Isle of Wight. RANGE: Bembridge Beds. [Syn., *Helix vectiensis*]

4. **Planorbina discus** (Edwards). (×1.) Bembridge Limestone, Sconce, Isle of Wight. RANGE: Headon–Hamstead Beds. [Syn., *Planorbis discus.*]

5.* **Tornatellaea simulata** (Solander). (×1½.) Upper Barton Beds, Barton, Hants. RANGE: London Clay–Barton Beds. [Syn., *Solidula simulata.*]

6. **Hemipleurotoma plebeia** (J. de C. Sowerby). (×1½.) Bracklesham Beds, Bracklesham Bay, Sussex. RANGE: Bracklesham–Headon Beds. [Syn., *Pleurotoma plebeia, P. denticula* of authors.]

7.* **Galba longiscata** (Brongniart). (×1.) Headon Beds, Headon Hill, Isle of Wight. RANGE: Headon–Bembridge Beds. [Syn., *Lymnaea longiscata.*]

8.* **Planorbina euomphalus** (J. Sowerby). (×1.) Headon Beds, Headon Hill, Isle of Wight. RANGE: Headon Beds. [Syn., *Planorbis euomphalus.*]

9. **Leptoconus edwardsi** (Cossmann). (×¾.) Upper Bracklesham Beds, Bramshaw, Hants. RANGE: Bracklesham Beds. [Syn., *Conus deperditus* Edwards.]

10.* **Hemiconus scabriculus** (Solander). (×1½.) Barton Beds, Barton, Hampshire.

11.* **Filholia elliptica** (J. Sowerby). (×½.) Bembridge Beds, Headon Hill, Isle of Wight. RANGE: Headon–Bembridge Beds. [Syn., *Bulimus ellipticus.*]

12. **Palaeoglandina costellata** (J. Sowerby). (×1.) Bembridge Limestone, Sconce, Isle of Wight. RANGE: Bembridge Beds. [Syn., *Bulimus costellatus.*]

Plate 27

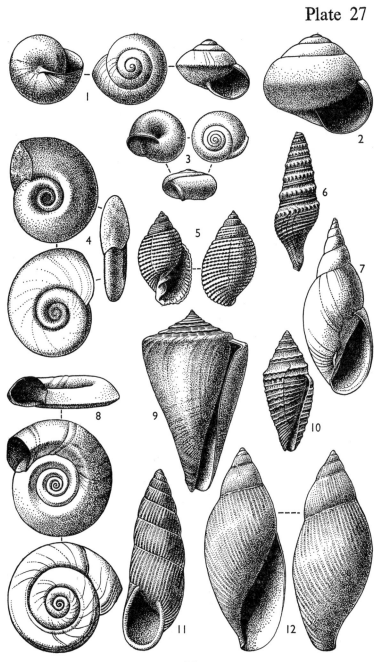

Plate 28

Eocene Sharks' Teeth (Figs. 1–6, 8–10), Cephalopods (Figs. 7, 12) and Scaphopod (Fig. 11)

1.* **Lamna obliqua** (Agassiz). (×1.) London Clay, Sheppey, Kent. RANGE: Thanet Sands–London Clay. [Syn., *Otodus obliquus*.]

2.* **Odontaspis (Synodontaspis) teretidens** White. (×1½.) Blackheath Beds, Abbey Wood, Kent. RANGE: Blackheath Beds–London Clay Basement Bed.

3.* **Striatolamia striata** (Winkler.) (×1½.) Blackheath Beds, Abbey Wood, Kent. RANGE: Thanet Sands–London Clay Basement Bed. [Syn. *Odontaspis elegans* of authors.]

4. **Galeorhinus minor** (Agassiz). (×2.) Barton Beds, Barton, Hants. RANGE: London Clay–Barton Beds. [Syn., *Galeocerdo minor*, *Eugaleus minor*.]

5. **Physodon secundus** (Winkler). (×2.) Lower Bracklesham Beds, Southampton, Hants. RANGE: London Clay–Barton Beds.

6. **Galeocerdo latidens** Agassiz. (×1½.) Lower Bracklesham Beds, Southampton, Hants. RANGE: Bracklesham–Barton Beds.

7.* **Belosaepia sepioidea** (Blainville). (×1.) Upper Bracklesham Beds, Bramshaw, Hants. RANGE: London Clay–Barton Beds.

8.* **Procarcharodon auriculatus** (Blainville), (×1.) Bracklesham Beds, Bracklesham, Sussex. RANGE: Bracklesham–Barton Beds.

9.* **Notidanus serratissimus** Agassiz. (×1½.) London Clay, Sheppey, Kent. RANGE: London Clay.

10. **Squatina prima** (Winkler). (×1½.) Blackheath Beds, Abbey Wood, Kent. RANGE: Woolwich–Barton Beds.

11.* **"Antalis striata"** (J. Sowerby). (×1.) Barton Beds, Barton, Hants. RANGE: Bracklesham–Barton Beds.

12.* **Cimomia imperalis** (J. Sowerby). (×¾.) The shell-wall has been broken away to show the internal septa. London Clay, Sheppey, Kent. RANGE: London Clay. [Syn., *Nautilus imperialis*.]

Plate 28

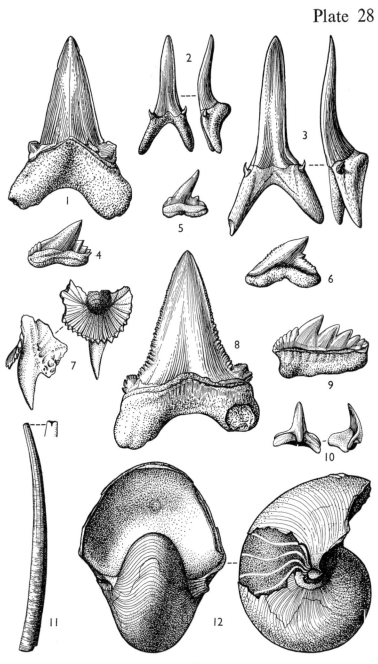

Plate 29

Eocene and Oligocene Fishes

1.* **Aetobatus irregularis** Agassiz. Eagle Ray. Lower tooth-plate. ($\times\frac{1}{2}$.) *a*, anterior edge; *b*, biting surface; *c*, attached surface. Lower Bracklesham Beds, Southampton, Hants. RANGE: London Clay–Barton Beds.

2.* **Myliobatis striatus** Buckland. Eagle Ray. Lower tooth-plate. ($\times\frac{1}{2}$.) *a*, anterior edge; *b*, attached surface; *c*, biting surface. Barton Beds, Highcliffe, Hants. RANGE: Bracklesham–Barton Beds.

3. **Hypolophus sylvestris** White. Tooth. ($\times 2$.) Blackheath Beds, Abbey Wood, Kent. RANGE: Blackheath Beds.

4.* **Acipenser** sp. Sturgeon. Lateral scute. ($\times 1$.) Lower Hamstead Beds, Hamstead, Isle of Wight. RANGE of genus: Upper Cretaceous –present day.

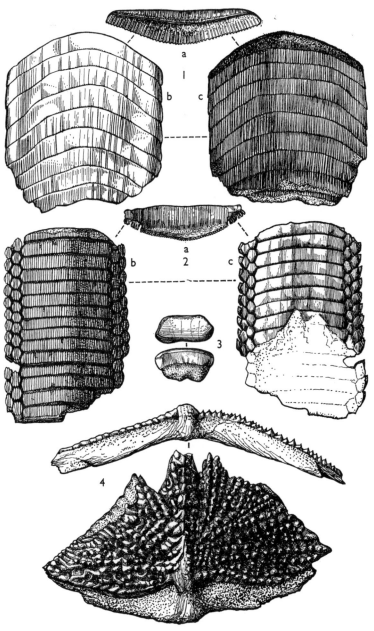

Plate 29

89

Plate 30

Eocene and Oligocene Fishes (Figs. 1–6), Reptiles (Figs. 7–10) and Mammals (Fig. 11)

1. **Phyllodus toliapicus** Agassiz. Upper pharyngeal dentition. ($\times 1$.) Blackheath Beds, Abbey Wood, Kent. RANGE: Woolwich Beds–London Clay.

2. **Edaphodon bucklandi** Agassiz. Mandibular tooth ($\times \frac{1}{2}$.) Bracklesham Beds.

3.* **Amia** sp. Opercular plate. ($\times 1$.) Bembridge Marls, Thorness Bay, Isle of Wight. RANGE of genus: Upper Cretaceous–present day (freshwater).

4.* **Albula eppsi** White & Frost. Otolith. ($\times 1$.) Blackheath Beds, Abbey Wood, Kent. RANGE: Blackheath Beds–London Clay Basement Bed.

5.* **Lepisosteus suessionensis** Gervais. Scale. ($\times 1$.) Blackheath Beds, Abbey Wood, Kent. RANGE: Blackheath Beds. [Syn., *Lepidosteus suessionensis*.]

6.* **Cylindracanthus rectus** (Dixon). Rostrum. ($\times \frac{1}{2}$.) Bracklesham Beds, Bracklesham, Sussex. RANGE: London Clay–Barton Beds.

7.* **Palaeophis toliapicus** Owen. Vertebra of Snake. ($\times 1$.) London Clay, Sheppey, Kent. RANGE: London Clay.

8, 9.* **Diplocynodon hantoniensis** (Wood). Crocodile. 8, tooth ($\times 1$); 9, dorsal vertebra ($\times \frac{1}{2}$). Lower Headon Beds, Hordle, Hants. RANGE: Lower Headon Beds.

10.* **Trionyx circumsulcatus** Owen. Costal bone of Turtle. ($\times \frac{1}{2}$.) Lower Headon Beds. Hordle, Hants. RANGE: Lower Headon Beds. [Syn., *Aulacochelys circumsulcatus*.]

11.* **Plagiolophus minor** (Cuvier). Upper molar of early relative of Horse. ($\times 1$.) Bembridge Beds, Isle of Wight. RANGE: Osborne–Bembridge Beds. [Syn., *Palaeotherium minus*].

Plate 30

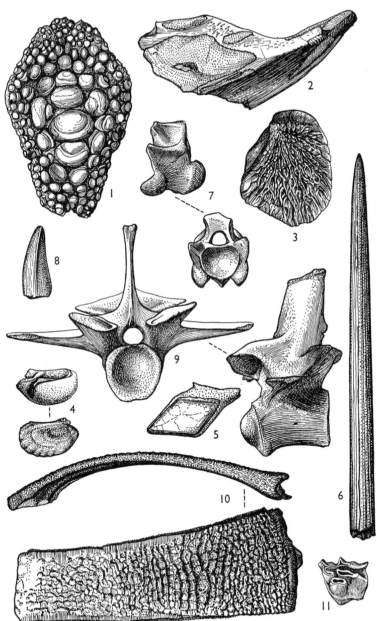

91

Plate 31

Pliocene and Quaternary Polyzoa (Fig. 1), Corals (Figs. 2, 4) and Sea-Urchin (Fig. 3)

1.* **Meandropora tubipora** (Busk). (*a*, ×1; b, ×5). Coralline Crag, Sudbourne, Suffolk. RANGE: Coralline Crag. [Syn., *Fascicularia tubipora*.]

2.* **Sphenotrochus intermedius** (Münster). (×3). Coralline Crag, Sutton, Suffolk. RANGE: Coralline Crag–Red Crag.

3.* **Echinocyamus pusillus** (Müller). (×3.) Red Crag, Alderton, Suffolk, RANGE: Red Crag–present day.

4.* **Balanophyllia caliculus** S. V. Wood. (×3.) Red Crag, Bentley, Suffolk. RANGE: Red Crag.

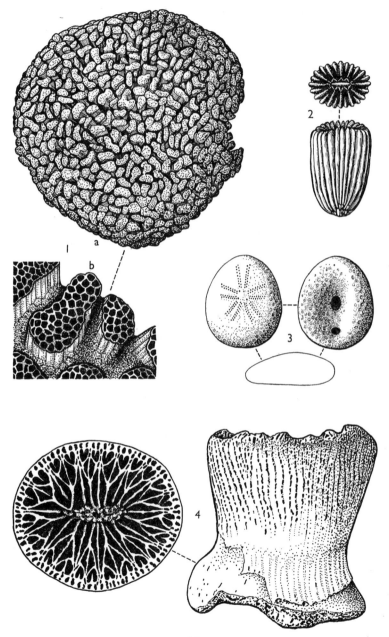

Plate 31

Plate 32

Pliocene and Quaternary Bivalve (Fig. 1)
Barnacle (Fig. 2), Brachiopod (Fig. 3), and Sea-Urchin (Fig. 4)

1.* **Yoldia oblongoides** (S. V. Wood). (×1.) Norwich Crag, Chillesford, Suffolk. RANGE: Red Crag–Corton Beds. [Syn., *Yoldia myalis*, *Leda myalis* of British authors.]

2.* **Balanus concavus** Bronn. Barnacle. (×1.) Coralline Crag, Sudbourne, Suffolk. RANGE: Coralline Crag–present day.

3.* **Terebratula maxima** Charlesworth. (×$\frac{1}{2}$.) Coralline Crag, Orford, Suffolk. RANGE: Coralline Crag.

4.* **Temnechinus excavatus** Forbes. (*a, b,* ×1$\frac{1}{2}$; *c,* ×5). Coralline Crag, Sutton, Suffolk. RANGE: Coralline Crag.

Plate 32

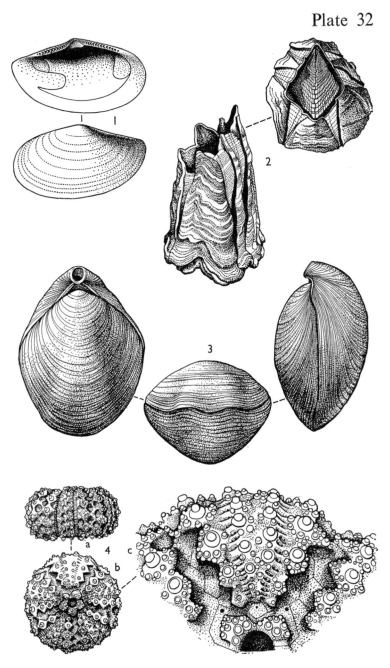

Plate 33

Pliocene and Quaternary Bivalves

1, 2. **Nucula laevigata** J. Sowerby. (×1.) Red Crag, Walton-on-Naze, Essex. RANGE: Red Crag.

3.* **Acila cobboldiae** (J. Sowerby). (×1.) Red Crag, Sutton, Suffolk. RANGE: Red Crag–Corton Beds. [Syn., *Nucula cobboldiae*.]

4, 5. **Chlamys (Palliolum) tigerina** (Müller). (4*a*, ×1½; 4*b*, ×4; 5, ×1½.) Coralline Crag, Ramsholt, Suffolk. RANGE: Coralline Crag–present day. [Syn., *Pecten tigrinus*.]

6.* **Glycymeris glycymeris** (Linné). Dog Cockle. (×¾.) Red Crag, Walton-on-Naze, Essex. RANGE: Coralline Crag–present day. [Syn., *Pectunculus glycymeris*.]

7, 8.* **Chlamys (Aequipecten) opercularis** (Linné). Quin. (×¾.) Coralline Crag, Sutton, Suffolk. RANGE: Coralline Crag–present day. [Syn., *Pecten opercularis*.]

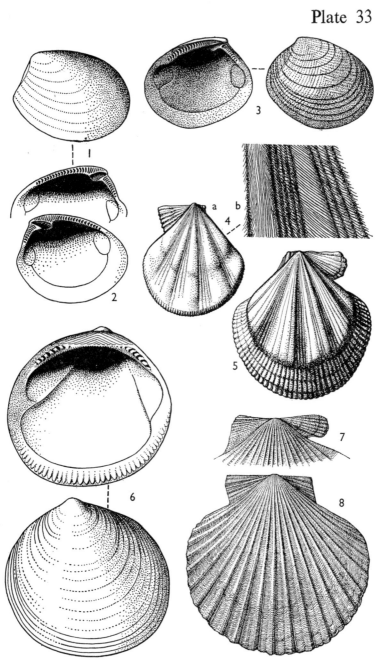

Plate 33

Plate 34
Pliocene and Quaternary Bivalves

1, 2.* **Pseudamussium gerardi** (Nyst). (×¾.) Coralline Crag, Gedgrave, Suffolk. RANGE: Coralline Crag. [Syn., *Pecten gerardi.*]

3, 4.* **Astarte obliquata** J. Sowerby. (×1.) Red Crag, Walton-on-Naze, Essex. RANGE: Red Crag.

5.* **Astarte semisulcata** (Leach). (×1.) Pleistocene, Bridlington, Yorks. RANGE in Britain: Norwich Crag–Clyde Beds; Arctic at present day. [Syn., *Astarte borealis* of authors.]

6. **Mytilus edulis** Linné. Common Mussel. (×¾.) Red Crag, Sutton, Suffolk. RANGE: Red Crag–present day.

7, 8. **Ostrea edulis** Linné. Oyster. (×½.) Coralline Crag, Suffolk. RANGE: Coralline Crag–present day.

Plate 34

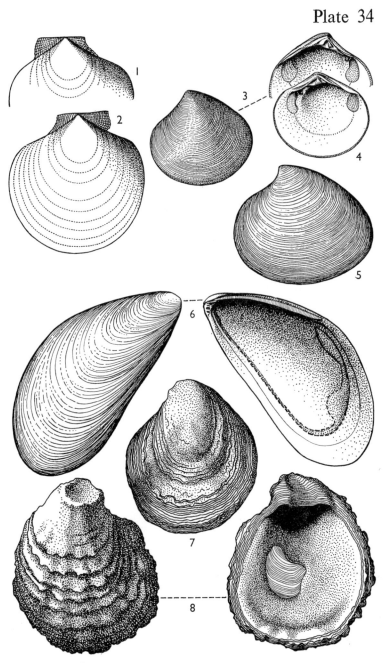

Plate 35

Pliocene and Quaternary Bivalves

1.* **Cardita senilis** (Lamarck). (×1.) Coralline Crag, Orford, Suffolk. RANGE: Coralline Crag–Red Crag.

2. **Cyclocardia scalaris** (J. Sowerby). (×2.) Red Crag, Ramsholt, Suffolk. RANGE: Coralline Crag–Corton Beds. [Syn., *Cardita scalaris.*]

3. **Astarte omalii** de la Jonkaire (×1.) Red Crag, Sutton, Suffolk. RANGE: Coralline Crag–Corton Beds.

4, 5.* **Arctica islandica** (Linné). (×¾.) Coralline Crag, Ramsholt, Suffolk. RANGE: Coralline Crag–present day. [Syn., *Cyprina islandica.*]

6. **Astarte mutabilis** S. V. Wood. (×1.) Coralline Crag, Sudbourne, Suffolk. RANGE: Coralline Crag–Red Crag.

7. **Digitaria digitaria** (Linné). (×2.) Red Crag, Little Oakley, Essex RANGE in Britain: Coralline Crag–Corton Beds; Mediterranean at present day. [Syn., *Astarte digitaria, Woodia digitaria.*]

8. **Pteromeris corbis** (Philippi). (×2.) Coralline Crag, Sutton, Suffolk. RANGE in Britain: Coralline Crag–Corton Beds; Mediterranean at present day. [Syn., *Cardita corbis.*]

Plate 35

101

Plate 36

Pliocene and Quaternary Bivalves

1, 2.* **Cardium (Acanthocardia) parkinsoni** J. Sowerby. (×¾.) Red Crag, Walton-on-Naze, Essex. RANGE: Red Crag.

3. **Cardium (Cerastoderma) edule** Linné. Common Cockle. (×¾.) Red Crag, Sutton, Suffolk. RANGE: Coralline Crag–present day.

4. **Cardium (Cerastoderma) angustatum** J. Sowerby. (×1.) Red Crag, Waldringfield, Suffolk. RANGE: Red Crag–Norwich Crag.

5–7.* **Phacoides (Lucinoma) borealis** (Linné). (×1.) Coralline Crag, Ramsholt, Suffolk. RANGE: Coralline Crag–present day. [Syn., *Lucina borealis*.]

8, 9. **Venus casina** Linné. (×1.) Red Crag, Sutton, Suffolk. RANGE: Coralline Crag–present day.

Plate 36

Plate 37

Pliocene and Quaternary Bivalves

1–3.* **Dosinia exoleta** (Linné). (×1.) Red Crag, Walton-on-Naze, Essex
RANGE: Red Crag–present day. [Syn., *Artemis exoleta.*]

4.* **Scrobicularia plana** (Da Costa). (×1.) Upper Pleistocene, Selsey
Bill, Sussex. RANGE: Red Crag–present day. [Syn., *Scrobicularia piperata* (Gmelin.)]

5.* **Spisula arcuata** (J. Sowerby). Trough Shell. (×¾.) Red Crag,
Walton-on-Naze, Essex: RANGE: Coralline Crag–Chillesford Beds.
[Syn., *Mactra arcuata.*]

Plate 37

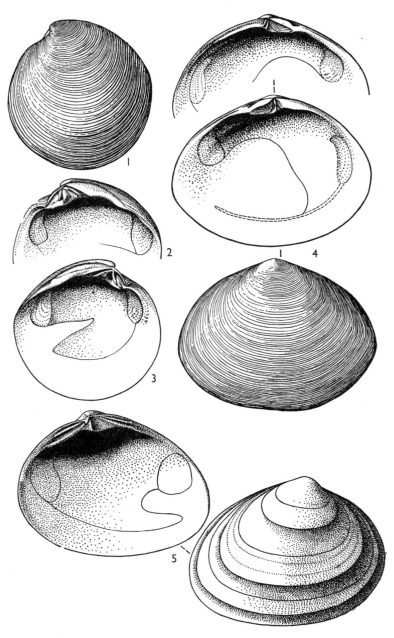

Plate 38

Pliocene and Quaternary Bivalves

1. **Macoma praetenuis** (Woodward). ($\times 1$.) Red Crag, Sutton, Suffolk. RANGE: Red Crag–Chillesford Beds. [Syn., *Tellina praetenuis*.]

2. **Macoma calcarea** (Gmelin). ($\times 1$.) Chillesford Beds, Chillesford, Suffolk. RANGE in Britain: Red Crag–Clyde Beds; Arctic at present day. [Syn., *Tellina calcarea, Tellina lata* Gmelin.]

3. **Spisula subtruncata** (Da Costa). ($\times 1$.) Norwich Crag, Yarn Hill, near Southwold, Suffolk. RANGE: Norwich Crag–present day. [Syn., *Mactra subtruncata*.]

4–6.* **Macoma balthica** (Linné). ($\times 1$.) "Shelly drift", Gloppa, near Oswestry, Shropshire. RANGE: Weybourne Crag–present day. [Syn., *Tellina balthica*.]

7–9.* **Macoma obliqua** (J. Sowerby). (7, $\times \frac{3}{4}$; 8, 9, $\times 2$). Red Crag, Sutton, Suffolk. RANGE: Coralline Crag–Corton Beds. [Syn., *Tellina obliqua.*]

10, 11. **Mya truncata** Linné. The Gaper. ($\times \frac{3}{4}$.) Coralline Crag, Ramsholt, Suffolk. RANGE: Coralline Crag–present day.

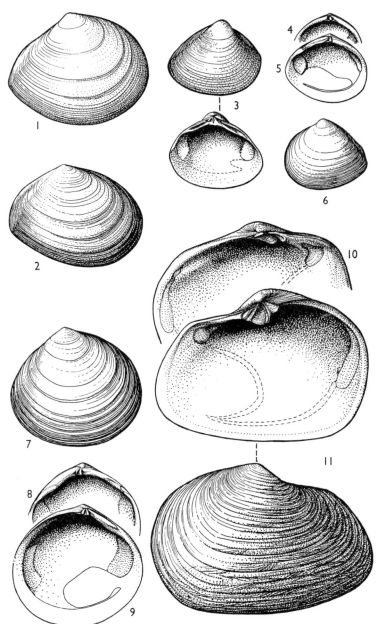

Plate 38

Plate 39
Pliocene and Quaternary Gastropods

1.* **Calliostoma subexcavatum** S. V. Wood. (×1.) Red Crag, Sutton, Suffolk. RANGE: Coralline Crag–Red Crag. [Syn., *Trochus subexcavatus.*]

2. **Emarginula reticulata** J. Sowerby. Slit Limpet. (×1½.) Red Crag, East Anglia. RANGE: Coralline Crag–present day. [Syn., *Emarginula fissura* of authors.]

3.* **Epitonium (Boreoscala) greenlandicum** (Perry). (×1.) Norwich Crag, Bramerton, Norfolk. RANGE: in Britain: Red Crag–Clyde Beds; Arctic at present day. [Syn., *Scala greenlandica, Scalaria greenlandica* of authors.]

4. **Hinia granulata** (J. Sowerby). (×3.) Red Crag, Walton-on-Naze, Essex. RANGE: Coralline Crag–Corton Beds. [Syn., *Nassa granulata.*]

5.* **Turritella (Haustator) incrassata** J. Sowerby. (×1.) Coralline Crag, Ramsholt, Suffolk. RANGE: Coralline Crag–Corton Beds.

6. **Turritella communis** Risso. Auger Shell. (×1.) Glacial deposits, Worden Hall, Lancashire. RANGE: Corton Beds–present day.

7, 8.* **Potamides tricinctus** (Brocchi). (×1.) 7, Red Crag, Sutton, Suffolk; 8, Norwich Crag, Yarn Hill, near Southwold, Suffolk. RANGE: Coralline Crag–Corton Beds. [Syn., *Cerithium tricinctum.*]

9. **Calyptraea chinensis** (Linné). Chinaman's Hat Limpet. (×1.) Coralline Crag, Gomer, near Gedgrave, Suffolk. RANGE: Coralline Crag–present day.

10.* **Trivia coccinelloides** (J. Sowerby). Cowry. (×1½.) Red Crag, Little Oakley, Essex. RANGE: Coralline Crag–Red Crag. [Syn., *Cypraea coccinelloides, Cypraea europaea* of authors.]

11. **Polinices hemiclausus** (J. Sowerby). (×1.) Red Crag, Walton-on-Naze, Essex. RANGE: Red Crag–Weybourne Crag. [Syn., *Natica hemiclausa.*]

12. **Capulus ungaricus** (Linné). Cap Shell. (×¾.) Red Crag, Walton-on-Naze, Essex. RANGE: Coralline Crag–present day.

13. **Natica multipunctata** S. V. Wood. (×1.) Red Crag, Walton-on-Naze, Essex. RANGE: Coralline Crag–Red Crag.

14. **Littorina littorea** (Linné). Winkle. (×1.) Red Crag, Sutton, Suffolk. RANGE: Red Crag–present day.

15. **Lunatia catenoides** (S. V. Wood). (×1.) Red Crag, Walton-on-Naze, Essex, RANGE: Coralline Crag–Red Crag. [Syn., *Natica catenoides.*]

Plate 39

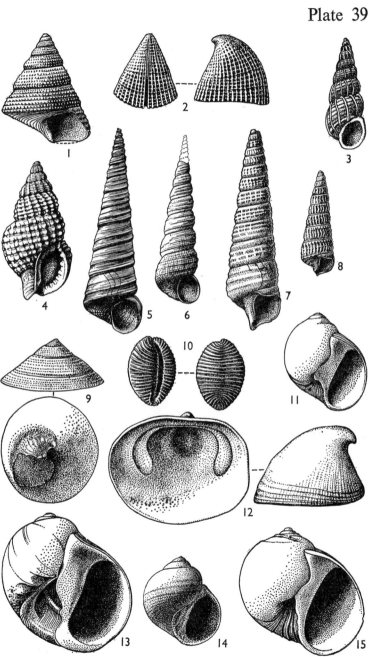

Plate 40

Pliocene and Quaternary Gastropods

1.* **Hinia reticosa** (J. Sowerby). (×1.) Red Crag, Walton-on-Naze, Essex. RANGE: Coralline Crag–Corton Beds. [Syn., *Nassa reticosa*.]

2. **Buccinum undatum** Linné. Whelk. (×¾.) Holocene clay, Belfast. RANGE: Red Crag–present day.

3.* **Trophonopsis (Boreotrophon) clathratus** (Linné). (×1.) Bridlington Crag, Bridlington, Yorks. RANGE in Britain: Coralline Crag–Corton Beds; Arctic at present day. [Syn., *Trophon scalariforme* (Gould).]

4.* **Leiomesus dalei** (J. Sowerby). (×1.) Red Crag, Walton-on-Naze, Essex. RANGE: Coralline Crag–present day. [Syn., *Buccinum dalei*.]

5.* **Neptunea despecta decemcostata** (Say). (×¾.) Red Crag, Little Oakley, Essex. RANGE in Britain: Red Crag–Norwich Crag; N.E. America at present day.

6.* **Searlesia costifera** (S. V. Wood). (×1.) Red Crag, Walton-on-Naze, Essex. RANGE in Britain: Coralline Crag–Red Crag; N. Atlantic at present day. [Syn., *Trophon costiferum*.]

7.* **Neptunea contraria** (Linné) (×½.) Red Crag, Walton-on-Naze, Essex. RANGE: Red Crag–late Pleistocene.

8.* **Nucella tetragona** (J. Sowerby). (×1.) Red Crag, Walton-on-Naze, Essex. RANGE: Coralline Crag–Red Crag. [Syn., *Purpura tetragona*.]

9.* **Sipho curtus** (Jeffreys). (×¾.) Red Crag, Ramsholt, Suffolk. RANGE: Red Crag. [Syn., *Fusus curtus*.]

Plate 40

Plate 41

Pliocene and Quaternary Marine Gastropods (Figs. 1, 5, 8, 14),
Freshwater Gastropods (Figs. 6, 7, 9–13, 15), Marine Fishes
(Figs. 2, 3), and Marine Mammal (Fig. 4)

1.* **Nucella incrassata** (J. Sowerby). Dog Winkle. (×1.) Red Crag, Sutton, Suffolk. RANGE: Red Crag–Corton Beds. [Syn., *Purpura incrassata, P. lapillus* of authors in part.]

2.* **Raja clavata** Linné. Dermal tubercle of Skate. (×1½.) Norwich Crag, Norwich, Norfolk. RANGE: Coralline Crag–present day.

3.* **Isurus hastalis** (Agassiz). Shark's tooth. (×1.) Red Crag, Woodbridge, Suffolk. RANGE: Coralline Crag–Red Crag.

4.* **Balaena affinis** Owen. Ear-bone of Whale. (×⅓.) Red Crag, Woodbridge, Suffolk. RANGE: Red Crag.

5.* **Scaphella lamberti** (J. Sowerby). (×1.) Red Crag, Walton-on-Naze, Essex. RANGE: Coralline Crag–Red Crag. [Syn., *Voluta lamberti.*]

6. **Ancylus fluviatilis** Müller. River Limpet. (×2.) Pleistocene (Hoxnian), Clacton, Essex. RANGE: Cromer Forest Bed–present day.

7. **Belgrandia marginata** (Michaud). (×9.) Pleistocene (Hoxnian), Clacton, Essex. RANGE in Britain: Cromerian–Upper Pleistocene; S. France at present day.

8. **Admete viridula** (Fabricius). (×1.) Red Crag, Suffolk. RANGE in Britain: Coralline Crag–Weybourne Crag; Arctic at present day. [Syn., *Cancellaria costellifera* S. V. Wood, *C. viridula.*]

9.* **Lymnaea (Radix) peregra** (Müller). Pond Snail. (×1.) Pleistocene (Hoxnian?), Ilford, Essex. RANGE: Red Crag–present day.

10. **Valvata antiqua** Morris. (×2½.) Pleistocene (Hoxnian), Swanscombe, Kent. RANGE: Middle Pleistocene.

11, 12. **Bithynia tentaculata** (Linné). Shell and operculum. (×2.) Pleistocene (Hoxnian), Swanscombe, Kent. RANGE: Norwich Crag–present day.

13.* **Viviparus diluvianus** (Kunth). River Snail. (×1.) Pleistocene (Hoxnian), Swanscombe, Kent. RANGE: Middle Pleistocene. [Syn., *Paludina diluviana, P. clactonensis* Wood.]

14. **Ringicula ventricosa** (J. de C. Sowerby). (×3.) Red Crag, Sutton, Suffolk. RANGE: Coralline Crag–Norwich Crag.

15.* **Planorbis planorbis** (Linné). Trumpet Snail. (×1½.) Pleistocene, West Wittering, Sussex. RANGE: Cromer Forest Bed–present day.

Plate 41

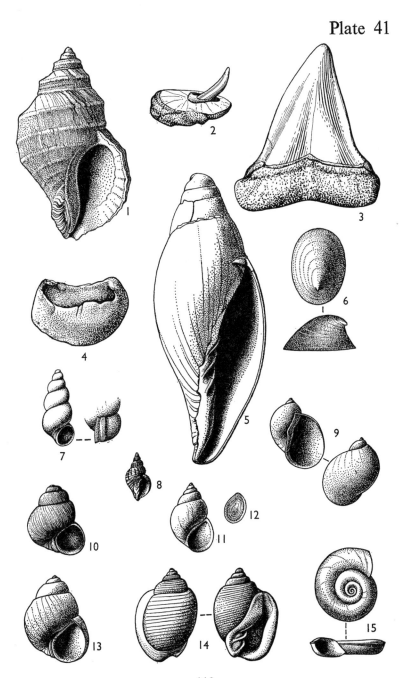

Plate 42

Quaternary Land Gastropods (Figs. 1–4) and Freshwater Bivalves (Figs. 5–9)

1. **Succinea oblonga** Draparnaud. Amber Snail. (× 3.) Pleistocene (Würmian), Tottenham, Middlesex. RANGE: Norwich Crag–present day.

2. **Hygromia (Trichia) hispida** (Linné). Bristly Snail. (× 3.) Holocene, Halling, Kent. RANGE: Red Crag–present day. [Syn., *Helix hispida*.]

3. **Pupilla muscorum** (Linné). (× 10.) Pleistocene (Würmian), Ponders End, Middlesex. RANGE: Red Crag–present day. [Syn., *Pupa muscorum, P. marginata* Draparnaud.]

4.* **Helix (Cepaea) nemoralis** Linné. (× 1.) Pleistocene (Hoxnian?,) Ilford, Essex. RANGE: Red Crag–present day.

5, 6.* **Unio (Potomida) littoralis** Cuvier. Freshwater Mussel. (× ¾.) Pleistocene (Hoxnian), Clacton, Essex. RANGE in Britain: Middle-Upper Pleistocene; European continent at present day.

7.* **Pisidium clessini** Neumayr. (× 4.) Pleistocene (Hoxnian), Swanscombe, Kent. RANGE: Norwich Crag–Upper Pleistocene. [Syn. *Pisidium astartoides* of authors.]

8, 9.* **Corbicula fluminalis** (Müller). (× 1.) Pleistocene (Eemian), Crayford, Kent. RANGE in Britain: Norwich Crag–Upper Pleistocene; N. Africa and Middle East at present day.

Plate 42

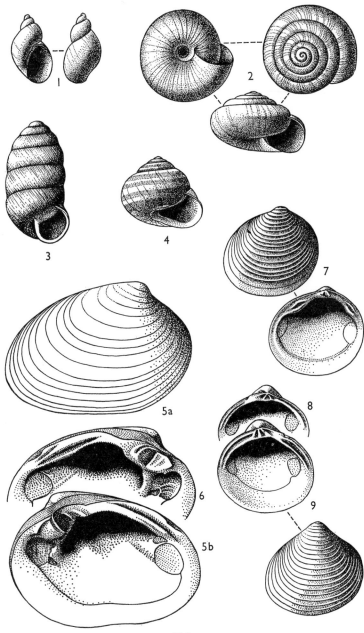

Plate 43

Quaternary Mammals

1, 2.* **Equus** sp. Horse. 1. Upper cheek tooth, *a*, side view and *b*, biting surface. ($\times \frac{1}{2}$.) Pleistocene, Felixstowe, Suffolk; 2. Lower cheek tooth, biting surface. ($\times \frac{1}{2}$.) Pleistocene, dredged off Happisburgh, Norfolk. RANGE: Lower Pleistocene–present day.

3, 4.* **Bos primigenius** Bojanus. Aurochs or Wild Ox. 3. Upper molar, biting surface. ($\times \frac{1}{2}$.) Upper Pleistocene, Walthamstow, Essex; 4. Third lower molar, *a*, biting surface and *b*, side view. ($\times \frac{1}{2}$.) Pleistocene, Kent's Cavern, Torquay, Devon. RANGE: Middle Pleistocene–Bronze Age; domesticated during Neolithic.

5.* **Coelodonta antiquitatis** (Blumenbach). Upper molar of Woolly Rhinoceros. ($\times \frac{1}{2}$.) Upper Pleistocene, Kent's Cavern, Torquay, Devon. RANGE: Middle–Upper Pleistocene. [Syn., *Rhinoceros antiquitatis, Tichorhinus antiquitatis, Rhinoceros tichorhinus* Cuvier.]

6.* **Hippopotamus amphibius** Linné. Molar of Hippopotamus. ($\times \frac{1}{2}$.) Pleistocene, near Bedford. RANGE: Lr. Pleistocene (Cromer Forest Bed)–Upper Pleistocene.

7. **Rangifer tarandus** (Linné.) Antler of Reindeer. ($\times \frac{1}{25}$.) Upper Pleistocene, Twickenham. Middlesex. RANGE: Middle–Upper Pleistocene.

8. **Cervus elaphus** Linné. Antler of Red Deer. ($\times \frac{1}{25}$.) Upper Pleistocene. Walthamstow, Essex. RANGE: Middle Pleistocene (Cromer Forest Bed)–present day.

9. **Megaceros giganteus** (Blumenbach). Antler of Irish Giant Deer. ($\times \frac{1}{25}$.) Pleistocene, Ireland. RANGE: Pleistocene. [Syn., *Cervus giganteus.*]

10. **Dama clactoniana** (Falconer). Antler of Clacton Fallow Deer. ($\times \frac{1}{25}$.) Middle Pleistocene, Swanscombe, Kent. RANGE: Middle–Upper Pleistocene. [Syn., *Cervus browni* Boyd Dawkins.]

Plate 43

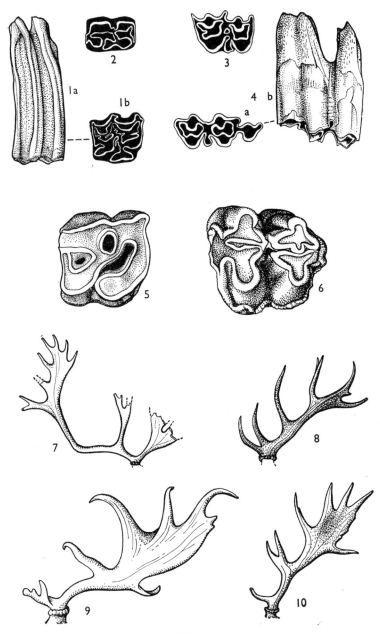

Plate 44

Pleistocene Mammals

1.* **Mammuthus primigenius** (Blumenbach). Wooly Mammoth. Upper molar biting surface. ($\times \frac{1}{4}$.) Upper Pleistocene, dredged from the Thames at Millbank, Westminster, London. RANGE: Upper Pleistocene. [Syn., *Elephas primigenius*.]

2.* **Anancus arvernensis** (Croizet and Jobert). Mastodon. Upper molar: *a*, side view; *b*, biting surface. ($\times \frac{1}{4}$.) Red Crag, Suffolk. RANGE: Lr. Pleistocene (Red Crag–Norwich Crag).

3.* **Palaeoloxodon antiquus** (Falconer and Cautley). Straight-tusked Elephant. Upper molar: *a*, side view; *b*, biting surface. (Both $\times \frac{1}{4}$.) Pleistocene, near Greenhithe, Kent. RANGE: Middle–Upper Pleistocene. [Syn., *Elephas antiquus*.]

4.* **Crocuta crocuta spelaea** (Goldfuss), Cave Hyaena, *a*, right lower jaw ($\times \frac{1}{4}$); *b*, biting surface of teeth of same specimen ($\times \frac{1}{4}$). Upper Pleistocene, Kent's Cavern, Torquay, Devon. RANGE: Middle–Upper Pleistocene. Extinct race, species still occurs in Africa. [Syn., *Hyaena spelaea*.]

5.* **Ursus deningeri** von Reichenau. Bear. *a*, left lower jaw ($\times \frac{1}{3}$); *b*, biting surface of teeth of same specimen ($\times \frac{1}{2}$). Cromer Forest Bed, Bacton, Norfolk. RANGE: Middle Pleistocene (Cromer Forest Bed).

Plate 44

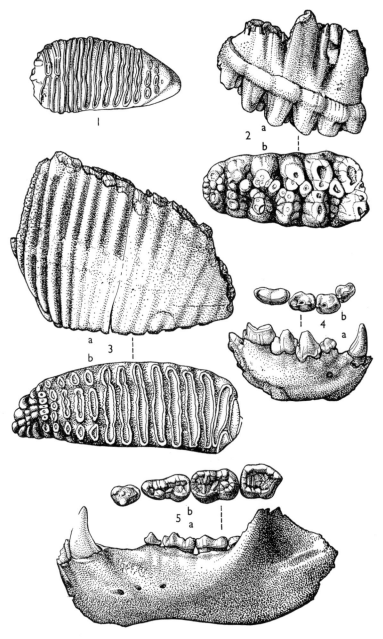

Bibliography

The following is a list of the most important works of reference, mainly illustrated monographs, in which further information on British Caenozoic fossils can be found.

BRITISH MUSEUM (NATURAL HISTORY) PUBLICATIONS

AZZAROLI, A. 1953. The Deer of the Weybourne Crag and Forest Bed of Norfolk. *Bulletin, Geology*, **1**, 1.

CASIER, E. 1966. *Faune Ichthyologique du London Clay.*

CHANDLER, M. E. J. 1957. The Oligocene Flora of the Bovey Tracey Lake basin, Devonshire. *Bulletin, Geology*, **3**, 3.

CHANDLER, M. E. J. 1960. *Lower Tertiary Flora of Southern England*, 1. *Palaeocene Floras. London Clay Flora (Supplement).*

CHANDLER, M. E. J. 1960. Plant Remains of the Hengistbury and Barton Beds. *Bulletin, Geology*, **4**, 6.

CHANDLER, M. E. J. 1961. Post-Ypresian Plant Remains from the Isle of Wight and the Selsey Peninsular, Sussex. *Bulletin, Geology*, **5**, 2.

CHANDLER, M. E. J. 1961. Flora of the Lower Headon Beds of Hampshire and the Isle of Wight. *Bulletin, Geology*, **5**, 5.

CHANDLER, M. E. J. 1963. Revision of the Oligocene Floras of the Isle of Wight. *Bulletin, Geology*, **6**, 3.

CHANDLER, M. E. J. 1962. *Lower Tertiary Floras of Southern England*, **2**. *Flora of the Pipe-clay Series of Dorset (Lower Bagshot.)*

CHANDLER, M. E. J. 1963. *Lower Tertiary Floras of Southern England*, **3**. *Flora of the Bournemouth Beds, the Boscombe and the Highcliff Sands.*

HINTON, M. A. C. 1926. *Monograph of Voles and Lemmings (Microtinae) Living and Extinct.* Vol. 1.

NEWTON, R. B. 1891. *Systematic List of the Frederick E. Edwards Collection of British Oligocene and Eocene Mollusca.*

REID, E. M., and CHANDLER, M. E. J. 1925. *The Bembridge Flora.*

REID, E. M., and CHANDLER, M. E. J. 1933. *The London Clay Flora.*

WHITE, E. I. 1931. *The Vertebrate Faunas of the English Eocene.* Vol. 1. *From the Thanet Sands to the Basement Beds of the London Clay.*

WITHERS, T. H. 1953. *Catalogue of Fossil Cirripedia.* Vol. 3. *Tertiary.*

PALAEONTOGRAPHICAL SOCIETY MONOGRAPHS

ADAMS, A. L. 1877–81. *Monograph on the British Fossil Elephants.*

BUSK, G. 1859. *A Monograph of the Fossil Polyzoa of the Crag.*

CHANDLER, M. E. J. 1925–6. *The Upper Eocene Flora of Hordle, Hants.*

DAVIDSON, T. *A Monograph of the British Fossil Brachiopoda.*
  1852. Vol. 1, part 1. *The Tertiary Brachiopoda.*
  1874. Vol. 4, part 1. *Supplement to the Recent, Tertiary and Cretaceous Species.*

DAWKINS, W. B., and SANFORD, W. A. 1866–72. *A Monograph of the British Pleistocene Mammalia.* Vol 1. *British Pleistocene Felidae.*

DUNCAN, P. M. 1866–91. *A Monograph of the British Fossil Corals.* Second Series.

EDWARDS, F. E. (continued by Wood S. V.). 1849–77. *A Monograph of the Eocene Cephalopoda and Univalves of England.* Vol. 1 [not completed].

EDWARDS, H. M., and HAIME, J. 1850–55. *A Monograph of the British Fossil Corals.*

FORBES, E. 1852. *Monograph of the Echinodermata of the British Tertiaries.*

GARDNER, J. S. 1883–86. *A Monograph of the British Eocene Flora.* Vol. 2. *Gymnospermae.*

GARDNER, J. S., and ETTINGSHAUSEN, C. von. 1879–82. *A Monograph of the British Eocene Flora.* Vol. 1. *Filices.*

HARMER, F. W. 1914–24. *The Pliocene Mollusca of Great Britain.*

JONES, T. R. 1857. *A Monograph of the Tertiary Entomostraca of England.*

JONES, T. R., and others, 1866–97. *A Monograph of the Foraminifera of the Crag.*

JONES, T. R., and SHERBORN, C. D. 1889. *A Supplementary Monograph of the Tertiary Entomostraca of England.*

OWEN, R., and BELL, T. 1849–58. *Monograph of the Fossil Reptilia of the London Clay and of the Bracklesham and other Tertiary beds.*

REYNOLDS, S. H. 1902–39. *A Monograph of the British Pleistocene Mammalia* Vols. 2 and 3.

WOOD, S. V. 1848–82. *A Monograph of the Crag Mollusca.*

WOOD, S. V. 1861–77. *A Monograph of the Eocene Bivalves of England* [not completed].

OTHER PUBLICATIONS

ADAMS, C. G. 1962. *Alveolina* from the Eocene of England. *Micropaleont.* New York, **8** : 45–54.

BOWEN, R. N. C. 1953. Ostracoda from the London Clay. *Proc. Geol. Assoc.,* London, **64** : 276–292.

BOWEN, R. N. C. 1953. Foraminifera from the London Clay. *Proc. Geol. Assoc.,* London, **65**: 125–174.

DIXON, F. 1850. *The Geology and Fossils of the Tertiary and Cretaceous Formations of Sussex,* London.

KENNARD, A. S., and WOODWARD, B. B. 1901. The Post Pliocene Non-marine Mollusca of the South of England. *Proc. Geol. Assoc.,* London, **17**: 213–260 and table. [Lists].

KENNARD, A. S., and WOODWARD, N. B. 1922. The Post Pliocene Non-marine Mollusca of the East of England. *Proc. Geol. Assoc.,* London, **33**: 104–142. [Lists].

MUIR-WOOD, H. M. 1938. Notes on British Eocene and Pliocene Terebratulas. *Annals and Magazine of Natural History,* London, (11) **2**: 154–181.

NEWTON, E. T. 1882. *The Vertebrata of the Forest Bed Series of Norfolk and Suffolk*, London. Memoir of the Geological Survey of England and Wales.

STINTON, F. C. 1956. Fish Otoliths from the London Clay of Bognor Regis, Sussex. *Proc. Geol. Assoc.*, London, **67**, 15–31.

WOODWARD, B. B. 1890. The Pleistocene (Non-marine) Mollusca of the London District. *Proc. Geol. Assoc.*, London, **11**: 335–388 and table. [Lists.]

WRIGLEY, A. 1925–53. Series of papers on English Eocene and Oligocene Gastropoda in *Proc. Malacological Soc. London*, **16–30**.

WRIGLEY, A. 1951. Some Eocene Serpulids. *Proc. Geol. Assoc.*, London, **62**: 177–202.

General Index

The number in bold type is the plate number. Reference should be made to the explanation of plates for the number of the figure. The page numbers refer to the faunal lists for the successive beds.

123

Index to Genera and Species

Names in current use are printed in **heavy** type. Synonyms, or discarded names, are in *italics*. Cross references to sub-genera are in ordinary type. The first figure, in **heavy** type (**1**) refers to the plate; the second, in ordinary type (1) to the figure.

125